Mental Models

Improving Decision Making Skills and Critical Thinking, Problems Solving, Increase Your Productivity

By

William Bell

© Copyright 2019 by William Bell

All rights reserved.

This document is geared towards providing exact and reliable information with regard to the topic and issue covered. The publication is sold with the idea that the publisher is not required to render accounting, officially permitted or otherwise qualified services. If advice is necessary, legal or professional, a practiced individual in the profession should be ordered.

From a Declaration of Principles which was accepted and approved equally by a Committee of the American Bar Association and a Committee of Publishers and Associations.

In no way is it legal to reproduce, duplicate, or transmit any part of this document in either electronic means or in printed format. Recording of this publication is strictly prohibited, and any storage of this document is not allowed unless with written permission from the publisher. All rights reserved.

The information provided herein is stated to be truthful and consistent, in that any liability, in terms of inattention or otherwise, by any usage or abuse of any policies, processes, or directions contained within is the solitary and utter responsibility of the recipient reader. Under no circumstances will any legal responsibility or blame be held against the publisher for any reparation, damages, or monetary loss due to the information herein, either directly or indirectly.

Respective authors own all copyrights not held by the publisher.

The information herein is offered for informational purposes solely and is universal as so. The presentation of the information is without a contract or any type of guarantee assurance.

The trademarks that are used are without any consent, and the publication of the trademark is without permission or backing by the trademark owner. All trademarks and brands within this book are for clarifying purposes only and are owned by the owners themselves, not affiliated with this document.

TABLE OF CONTENTS

INTRODUCTION   7

Understanding Your Mental Model   12

Are Your Mental Models on the Low or High Road? 15

Effects of Thinking Pattern on Life   23

The Best Way to Simplify Thinking   27

The Art of Creative Thinking   49

Systems Thinking Basic Concept   60

Critical Thinking Concept   72

How Important Is Critical Thinking?   97

Critical Thinking -Things to Stay Away from Doing 103

Positive Thinking   112

Whole Brain Thinking for Businesspeople   120

Logical Thinking - Can It Be Bad or Good?   126

Prosperity" Thinking and How Can I Believe that Way?
-   130

Strategic Thinking	*136*
Energetic Thinking	*141*
Higher-Order Thinking	*148*
Thinking Outside of the Tightest Box	*155*
Mental Models for Learning Organizations	*161*
Mental Modeling and Thought Chains	*170*
Think Highly of Yourself	*175*
Mental Models: The Box Everyone Is Trying to Think Outside Of	*179*
Thinking of How We Think	*183*
CONCLUSION	*191*

INTRODUCTION

Y ou might have read the expression, "What you see is the thing that you get." It means that our view of the world inhibits our ability to experience it. Very few would argue with the reality that an individual that has ever experienced like in their lives has a good deal of trouble finding, maintaining, or sustaining a first-class connection.

Equivalently, if you have grown up in abject poverty, it requires a good deal of individual transformation before you can deal with abundance easily.

This particular book explores the similarities between the mystic tradition of "the energy of the mind" and the organizational or scientific advancement tradition of "mental models." All of us would like something. Playing with such ideas leads us down the highway, where we are more apt to buy it.

I will start our comparison of the power of the brain with a bit and mental models tory. As a long-held mystic tradition that you might know of implies, the ability to transform lead to gold handles the ability to alter an experience that is major laden to the one filled with abundance and potential with ideas transformation.

Changing the negative to the positive making use of our mind potential is a subject that surfaces periodically via human history. The widespread and recent most type continues to be the film The Secret and the proliferation of some excellent coaches, like Jerry and Esther Hicks.

Those who are working together with the potential of the brain build upon the concept that the' subconscious' may also permit us being in contact with the life force of the universe.

Through meditation and other processes that open our consciousness to more than what we are conscious of in our limited form, we will have access to suggestions that take our lives in unexpected and new directions.

Jerry and Esther Hicks pour the emotion to this particular blend and instruct us that our' emotional assistance system' usually allows us to know when we are on course with ourselves if we expertise happiness and weightlessness in our lives.

Mental versions may be traced to the job of Kenneth Craik in 1943 as he recommended the human brain constructs small scale versions of truth it uses to foresee activities. He proceeded to propose that the mental model is often built from perception, our imagination, or the norms of the life we lead on the occasions we live.

The intriguing point here is that mental models tie carefully to visual images and could be abstract. Have you checked out a design of someone's idea, and "get it "instantly? That is the power of the mental model.

Jay W. Forrester defined it as: "The picture of the earth around us that we have in our head is a model that nobody imagines all the world, country, or government. He's selected principles, and relationships between them, and requires all to stand for the actual system."

Mental models are greatly ingrained assumptions, generalizations, or perhaps photos or pictures that affect how we understand the world and how we do something. What is common to both these is the thought that until we recognize the boundaries of our thinking or mental models, we cannot alter them.

Once aware, our ability to take action on new ideas is significantly enhanced.

Regardless if we phrase it the strength of mind or a mental style, our first step is recognizing the constraints we have in our lives as a result of how we think.

As we couldn't have dreamed the lives that we very quickly living nowadays associated with individuals with the world a mere thirty years back, we have to start to the concept that the possibility that life might be a lot more vast and a lot more fascinating than we can picture these days.

Jerry and Esther Hicks will remind us that if we are embroiled in things that do not feel great, we are out of connection with our highest potential. The individuals that are working with corporate mental models also suggest that if we cannot get past how we believe right now, we will be equipped to open up to the new potentials all around.

My question is: How can we focus our mental models, or our potential of the minds, to produce that?

This particular Guide is completely packaged together with the best basic thinking principles to offer the ideal solution to this question.

Let us get started.

CHAPTER 1

Understanding Your Mental Model

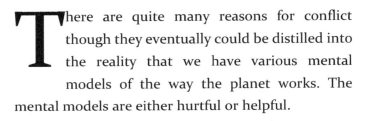

There are quite many reasons for conflict though they eventually could be distilled into the reality that we have various mental models of the way the planet works. The mental models are either hurtful or helpful.

On the one hand, they are extremely useful in how they protect us and simplify our lives from the power of being forced to rethink each view we have every time we are confronted with a situation.

These designs tend to be contextual. We have various versions for every facet of daily life, from whom we choose to be buddies with, to what music type we pay attention to, to the sorts of foods we consume, and the make of automobile we drive.

Your parameters and mental model for restaurant selection could be the restaurant use locally grown produce and have a vegetarian selection largely at reasonable prices. Your friend may have a mental design that dictates they dine in expensive restaurants with the finest wines and choicest cuts of beef.

These are the exact opposite ends of the spectrum, and thus there isn't much of a compromise for the folks in one or the other end at discovering an area they can dine together (i.e., the monetary element by itself is, in essence, a deal-breaker when neither is prepared to budge).

Or take, for instance, your choice in where you reside. One individual wishes to dwell in a metropolitan area surrounded by exercise, galleries, restaurants, theater, shops, and variety, and their partner wants to live in a small or rural t environment where there is lawn between the homes and one-stop sign in the city.

We do not understand purposely that these mental models will be in motion up until we come up against somebody who has opposite mental models. If you are among like-minded individuals in an isolated environment, you can surely stay away from the expertise of individually understanding other versions of the world are attainable.

It is not that you do not recognize these other values are out there; nonetheless, since you understand variations of trust are available at least based on tv, movies, and the web.

Problems arise when we are not conscious of our mental models. We can get stuck and be stubborn and believe ours will be the sole way. I have noticed this occur with more mature people in my family -- there are a right way and a wrong manner, so that is how it is.

They believe that there is one strategy for the world to do the job, and the issues of the world lay in the noncompliance of everyone who does not share their world view.

That might be a remarkably big burden to become the keeper of the reality regarding the way the world works. How does this match into persuasion?

Effectively, that falls under the heading of understanding thyself. When we excavate our mental models, we can overturn engineer where things are not working, or if they are working, we can reverse engineer to determine how we have become very effective at what we manifest.

CHAPTER 2

Are Your Mental Models
on the Low or High Road?

Mental versions will be described as "generalizations, deeply ingrained assumptions, and photos of pictures that affect how we bring an action and understand the world."

Mental models do have a substantial effect on how we see, respond to, and react to the world; they condition our quality-of-life, relationships, and decisions. They affect us on almost all levels - personal, organizational, professional, social, global, and national.

My purpose is raising your level of understanding of what mental models are and the way they operate. Useful neuroscience principles and tools allow you to challenge, change, and control your mental models for a better, more peaceful, and less stressful life.

Private Observations

- Mental models are saved info and mental imprints of the way your mind perceived and remembered immediate individual experiences and info learned from a third party or indirect tool such as the press.

- Models that will yield harmful outcomes for you and others are excellent candidates for examination and altered thinking.

- Formed over time from amassed info, they might be created deeply and quickly based on their importance and mental impact.

- Most individuals are ignorant of their models, wherever they came from, and their effects.

- They are challenging and subtle to identify and describe.

- They appear to run in a "backroom" or subconscious part of our brain.

- Our models often get stronger with time as human nature would like to be "right" regarding their opinions.

○ They may or might not be verifiable through independent observations or direct experience from integrous people.

I think the core issue is "how rightly do the mental models work me and others," rather than "are my mental versions appropriate or wrong?" There is no right way of consuming and processing sensory info because everybody perceives and interprets info differently.

A group of individuals agreeing on one thing does not make it real; the procedure binds the group around what they hold to be real. Needless arguments and wars ensue because of variations of opinion regarding mental models.

Evaluating

These daily life situations provide you with a grasp of what mental models seem like; each pair has variations of mindset for illustrative purposes. As you look them over, think about which ones may serve you and some best, instead of choosing what could be accurate or in errors.

The goal of this exercise is shifting your focus to a "high road" or a good perspective for evaluating mental models. With luck, these examples will stimulate your thinking to write down the mental models that serve you poorly or well.

Minimal Road: Good ideas for development are drying up, and there is a restricted business opportunity for me to prosper.

High Road: Good ideas for new products, technology, and services are infinite and endless.

_____

_____

_____

Low Road: We are now living in a competitive world of scarcity.

Great Road: We are now living in a world of boundless opportunity where by situational cooperation is achievable.

_____

_____

_____

Low Road: Girls do badly on science and math.

Higher Road: Anyone can discover what interests her or him, when in a supportive atmosphere.

_____

_____

_____

Low Road: You cannot believe in who appears to be, act and talk a particular way.

Higher Road: There are untrustworthy and trustworthy individuals in all areas of life.

_____

_____

_____

Low Road: In this economic system, nobody will interview me, a lot less, hire me.

Great Road: I have positive traits and transferable skills that some employer is searching for.

_____

_____

_____

Low Road: I cannot believe in myself behind the controls as a result of my driving record and even what my spouse says.

Higher Road: A renewal course will make me a more secure, more reliable and far better protective driver.

_____

_____

_____

Low Road: I cannot learn things that are new since I created bad grades and my teacher stated I was dumb.

High Road: My brain has infinite capacity to develop, get stronger, considered fast and make excellent decisions.

_____

_____

_____

Low Road: It is not likely I will live beyond 73 due to my family health history.

High Road: A healthy body practices and an optimistic mental attitude will increase my quality-of-life and maybe add years to my life span.

Mental models are what we feel and hold to be accurate about life. They are our "software programming" that drives thinking, behaviors, and opinions. There is usually an outcome from every mental model, although they might not be apparent. Individuals vehemently agree and disagree on the reality of their mental models.

The defining moment for challenging a mental model happens once the emphasis shifts to the preferred result. Clarity can best be accomplished by examining gaps between what is desired and the outcome that occurs. This is the sole way I know breaking the endless cycle of protecting and attacking mental models.

CHAPTER 3

Effects of Thinking Pattern on Life

The concept and meaning of life are fascinating topics of discussion. How we view it, at the start, is a place to ponder. What is becoming transpired and conspired, after birth to the end, is the passage, we experience in multi-dimensional mode. The multitude and variance of ideas reflect a considerable amount of people's heads and their thinking patterns.

The significance of life is a philosophical entity inside the idea of performance and existence. Our existence of accountability is directly proportional to our expectations and commitments. We are needed to meet obligations inside the ambit of dos and don'ts.

You will find regulations, rules, and guidelines imposed on human beings once we accept our realities and existence. There is no room for hypothetical deductions or fantasies. On the other hand, facts and factuality are life design. The life span is going in a manner as created by us.

The creational truth comprehensively balances between effect and cause. A unique takes its lead from knowledge and wisdom, a present from the creator. Today, the action and response reflect an individual's thinking design.

It adversely affects are encountered by individuals while in the passage of life span. It leaves its significant consequences clearly and distinctly. Nevertheless, few understand its implication, and some ignore it. A question comes up regarding the reason these anomalies surface when realities are open, and factuality appeared?

When specifics and phenomenon are open, a person or team ignores it in spite of sufficient evidence, subsequently arrogant sets in. Consequently, all the ill effects appear as beneficial and glorious. Hence, they get taken away into chaos and commotion, accepting the useful realities.

Thus, the thinking design of a private dictates its terms and compels him or her to acknowledge the impression as realities. This is an essential status, and one should exercise caution and get the utmost care.

If she or he succeeds, therefore, experiencing contentment and bliss.

The after-effect of the series of thinking indicates and advises that evaluating the problem must be the priority. You will find some smart males that think twice before making a choice and react.

The crucial point of the matter may be the culmination of ideas, and they are a center point of the design of thinking. At this point, the reactionary forces might produce hurdles that affect the type of thinking; thus, it impacts our life differently.

The reality is based on the realities of living as experienced by folks they accept it. The denial will be the negativity and stubbornness of a person deliberately relegating factuality and facts. Thus, the thinking design of a person is governed by two factors.

The straight forward path of truth leaves an advantageous effect on the life of a person. On the flip side, an arrogant individual's line of thinking and method is grounded on deception and falsehood. He thrives on fantasies and gets into delusion.

The crux of the topic is the improvement of mind enabling a regular individual to take control line of thinking. It usually thrives on some fundamental problems of cognition, emotions, or violation and feelings. Individuals and then get affected appropriately subject to environments and situations. They believe that things are designed to suit their desires.

They behave violently when encountering failures or denial. These are the peripheral perceptional tendencies. Nevertheless, a person apart from a regular person will react differently because of the ability to evaluate and look at the scenario in actualities and realities. He views outside of the horizon and appreciates the unforeseen and visible consequences in real terms relegating fantasies behind.

CHAPTER 4

The Best Way to Simplify Thinking

———⌒⟨·⟩⌒———

We face difficulties in daily life, particularly when we must think rather than accepting. All of us ask: Can we simplify our life?

Will we discover one easy and adequate idea for analyzing, controlling, and innovating everything and anything?

Can we solve some problems or gain any competition using one simple concept?

Have you wondered when we might lower everything to one idea?

With such questions, I spent the last several years examining our thinking and our economic and social circumstances. Through observing my thinking, discussing with individuals their problems, and studying formal reason and psychology, I discovered the following ideas well worth sharing.

For any company of life, my point of view is, every exercise is based on several typical factors. If perhaps

Mental Models | 27

we can comprehend those typical points contained in any task, we can surely stay away from errors and make success particular. But what is meant by these typical points? I am going to try to describe it briefly.

Inactivity, space, time, group, person, or anything, whatever is similar, saying, between, is the typical point. Something typical over time or across space is a typical point.

Anything typical among individual work or in collective initiatives is a typical point. Therefore in any task in all areas of life or virtually any maneuver, the matter that plays the main role is the common thing in that task.

For greater understanding, we can claim that, however, much produces a relation amongst items by linking them, establishes communication between them, as an outcome of what some activity comes into existence is the typical point.

For instance, in virtually any business entity, the character of the leader of the company is the typical point. The leader with the charming personality and competencies and abilities not binds the staff together but motivates the staff to work harder as an outcome of that the organization progresses, and the company earns a higher income.

Despite this, if the character of the leader is poor, no matter the best of high skill and plans of labor, the result will likely be the opposite.

People compete for things that they think about having value. There is a typical point or agreement that food is of value well worth expenditure. Despite this, folks cooperate when confronted with a mutual threat. This particular mutual threat is a typical point.

Like you have nerves in the body that link each a part of the body with the mind, they are taking signals from body to commands and brain from mind to body, then act as a widespread thing between brain and body, you

can find typical areas in virtually any method, setup, or organization. Through the awareness of these areas, we can evaluate, organize, or innovate the current structure. The most crucial devices in our life are our minds.

In virtually any sphere of daily life, our choices shape our lives. These decisions are derived from our thinking and our analysis of the scenario. Consequently, it is our thinking that shapes our life. In this particular view, the most essential activity in our life is thinking.

Thinking for examining situations, and innovating new results. If perhaps we can present the benefits of typical points, show they play a central role in the thinking, we can likewise demonstrate their importance in every struggle of living.

Let us observe one thing we all went through during the last couple of minutes.

As you are listening to this, your mind is processing this info.

Did it happen that while hearing this, you heard of some word, sentence, or phrase that reminded you of something more substantial? It took place. Did it not?

Even though you had heard this particular lecture, an integral part of this specific lecture created you remember one thing different, perhaps irrelevant.

It will happen a lot. When you listen, read, view one factor, an additional thought arises in your mind, so the main reason it comes is the fact that your brain picks a component of what you are purposely monitoring and forms a bridge between your conscious observation and then another thing in mind.

Let us undergo another illustration to clarify this. Let us point out, your friend remarks about the newness of new fruits if you both are in the market. This concept of' new' allows you to remember that another friend asked you to purchase a fresh cake for the party. But the' cake' is sweet; therefore, you remember.

And eating' sweet' could induce trouble for your' diabetes' and for keeping your' diabetes' in check, you need to take' medicine' often.

Nevertheless, you remember that your particular' drug' is intending to end and you should' buy more medicine.' For' purchasing a lot more medicine,' you choose to travel to the nearest healthcare store after buying the fruits in this marketplace.

This particular voyage of views from the newness of fruit to choosing to travel to a healthcare shop was possible with some tips that formed a bridge.

Every time you run into a concept, an element of the idea helps you remember another idea. In the above examples, they are' new," cake," sweet," diabetes," take medicine,' and' buy medicine.' These suggestions form a bridge between the existing notion and the following immediate concept.

Mental Models | 31

Separately, they are typical factors between the two following suggestions, and together they are ordinary things between two remote opinions of' newness' and' driving.'

This is how we move from one strategy to yet another. This is the fluidity of creativity. It is, likewise, a compelling approach to creative thinking.

In this particular illustration, we had remembered items, though we can confuse conditions, merge them, and build new ones in the same manner. For instance, think elf creating a cup of tea. You add hot water, a tea bag in addition to sugar for a cup. From' hot water,' you remember drinking' lemon' with warm water yesterday because the first time that had been an excellent experience.

Returning to tea, you choose to then add lemon in this particular mixture of warm water with tea. You wind up generating a new tea for you. It is black tea with orange. The typical point' hot water' helped you connect two opinions of black tea and orange that had been at first different.

It is the same way somebody innovated mobile cell phones with a digital camera by watching the common trait that each may be held in hand. This particular handheld feature was the typical point; he observed the feature by chance or as a result of the drive to take and send a picture to a loved one via phone. Nevertheless, this typical issue enabled him to mix two devices.

Had digicams being massive such as automobiles, or had the common thing among camera and mobile stayed unobserved, you'd ever take selfies. How unfortunate would that be? And so when you bring selfies, always remember common areas and their power to innovate and invent.

But maybe the application of common areas restricted to memory recall, innovation, and? No. It includes logic, critical thinking, and analysis of observation.

Like the fluidity, and memory recall, our concepts are overlapping and mixed. Several ideas that are a part of broader ideas can quickly form a bridge between two more general approaches. In several instances, they can develop a bridge between opposing thoughts and help us to flip the argument against its proponent.

For instance, someone argues that' Everyone has the flexibility to do anything he or she wants. Thus, there mustn't be some restrictions in all'. Because of this argument, it makes sense that a person isn't restricted from suppressing the independence of others.

Therefore, as an outcome, the odds are that there'll be no less than one person who won't have the flexibility to do one factor he or she wishes. This contradicts the case that everybody has the flexibility to do whatever he or she wants.

As we can observe, the concept that' one isn't restricted from suppressing independence of others' follows out of the conclusion of argument' there mustn't be some limitations in all' and connects it with the complete opposite of the idea of argument' Everyone has the flexibility to do anything he or she wishes'. As a result, it is typically between two different concepts.

This is the reason several philosophers earlier remarked: Every thesis has seeds negation. Hence any argument might be switched on its head by determining anything in the premises of the argument and utilizing it to develop a realization that contradicts an original argument.

Though the job of common areas extends beyond basic negation, they cause arguments and allow conclusions. For instance, I say: Tech businesses are hiring AI professionals nowadays. Most AI professionals are experts in the right thinking.

Thus, tech businesses are hiring specialists of right thinking. By becoming typical between two opinions of Tech companies hiring and specialist of right thinking, the terms' AI expert' allows us to conclude a thing regarding the relation of these two ideas.

Nevertheless, due to their absolute power, the common points might be deceptive. Imagine an additional argument: Knowledge is power. Energy will corrupt. Thus, knowledge corrupts.

Here evidently, the word' power' is a typical point though it has been used in two various meanings. The energy that corrupts is power more than people, and power coming from knowledge is power more than one's very weaknesses. Thus, it is not a typical between the two ideas.

Unwary of this dual significance, a person could be deceived into believing expertise is corrupt. This method of argumentation is used by fanatic leaders, mainly religious.

Consequently, for crystal clear thinking that we need to do to shape our lives better, we should identify and refine our understanding of typical areas in any argument. For analyzing some argument, we should concentrate on the typical factors in it; we have to find their absence and presence, their uses, and definitions.

The same as there can be the same idea typical between two principles that allow inference, sometime we may find similarities typical between two items to conclude something. This is called analogies. For instance, this particular presentation is getting a long love river Nile.

This particular length is the common characteristic between the two - my Nile and presentation. Consequently, because of similarity, it could be realized that I am going to talk a lot more.

Nevertheless, a great presentation needs to be as a women's skirt, long adequate to cover the topic and short adequate to create interest. Consequently, we can conclude that I am going to finish it quickly. Though we will see what inference is right, and that analogy worked in.

Inside analogies also, typical areas of similarities allow us to conclude, and consequently, these could be deceptive too. We must subsequently be cautious when establishing similarities.

Not similarities between two things, but a design that is typical across many conditions helps us classify things or make abstractions. For instance, we observe the creatures that breastfeed give birth rather compared to lay eggs.

Hence we generalize that most creatures that breastfeed give birth. Although a breast-feeding pet might lay an egg. For instance, Duck-billed platypus. Consequently, common traits or common points allow us to generalize, but caution is required.

Similarly, if a style is typical over time, it could be helpful for forecasting or could indicate the relation of effect and cause.

For instance, every time the core bank announces one thing economic market shows elevated volatility. One could suggest the announcements are because of increased volatility. Nevertheless, such generalizations are suggestive and barely conclusive.

This particular way our whole thinking, the foundation of life, since our thinking shapes our life, only works due to suggestions that create a bridge, same suggestions that are same, similar, or are repeating. These are common between other ideas. Thus, these are common points. It is these typical

Mental Models | 37

points that make us remember, classify, innovate, deduce, or infer.

In a nutshell, think of a chain-linked with a stone. Each website link of the chain makes sure that the whole chain acts as one unit and allows you to pull the stone in an ideal direction.

Nevertheless, if even one website link in the chain breaks, you won't have the ability to move the stone. Much love these links of the chain, relations, actions, thoughts, systems, or something is dependent on the areas that allow a link between two or more areas. These links are routine areas.

And much love each link of chain links with an immediate subsequent link, typical point's link with fast then one. A lack of common things between two points means they can't come together with such a product.

Everyday areas govern our thinking. Nevertheless, we can consciously evaluate them for staying away from some mistakes, and for entirely managing and deliberately innovating new outcomes.

The same as we inhale effortlessly, though we can intentionally alter the rhythm of breathing to get sure mental status, we can deliberately make use of the typical points, that currently apply effortlessly, to attain our goals.

By purposely watching the typical factors, improving them, controlling them, and innovating them, we can evaluate, control, and innovate everything and anything. We simplify. We decrease every situation to one concept. The concept of typical points. That is whatever is identical, similar, saying, and it is in between two or over issues, actions, ideas, or time.

As the typical areas play the main part in your thinking, and our thinking shapes your life, it is essential to evaluate the common points in every sphere of living also. Hence for problem-solving, we have to refine your understanding of the typical factors.

Today the question we have to answer is one question: What are the typical points in your present problem situation?

For answering this question, we have to concentrate on four principles. We will go through these four ideas right now, before describing seven actions required to apply the device for analyzing, controlling, or innovating via everyday areas.

To begin with, we observe items that are typical across individuals or time since they are repeating, either over time or across people. For instance, you want to advertise your product.

And you observe that each time there is a football match, nearly all of the individuals gather about television, even people who wouldn't watch. Consequently, you can employ this particular repetition over time that is predictable, for advertising your product to many individuals.

Furthermore, you might see a repeating pattern among young people in a space. You considered their desire to understand music. If perhaps you understand music, you have noticed a possible manner, sometimes to interact with them, and to promote them a few lessons.

Today one more thing is finding anyone or anything that is typically between two or more others. For instance, the intermediaries like wholesalers of merchandise marketplace exist between the producers and buyers. They connect the two, which is a positive function.

Nevertheless, they hoard to raise the rates that are negative function. A government regulation improved subsidy or tax that impacts these intermediaries will affect both producers and buyers indirectly as the intermediaries will modify their behavior appropriately.

Then you might today observe things that are the same. For instance, you might discover that the same individual who is your neighbor is part of a research organization you want to join. You can question him to guide you and maybe help you to be a part. This particular individual is, thus, prevalent between you and the group you want to join.

Like the same, another idea is akin. Similarities permit analogies that are strong ways for communicating feelings or ideas to people who haven't experienced them or for understanding elements of any pain much like another.

A good example of analogies is poetry. Faiz, a poet through Asia, is acknowledged for his use of analogies. He published a poem for his beloved, expressing how he missed her. He stated, in the desert of solitude,quiver the shadows of your voice, my love, the mirage of your lips.

By utilizing the analogies of wasteland, quivering, and mirage, he showed how he missed his beloved in a manner that, currently, anybody who realizes the typical point of the desert, mirage, and quiver can understand the intense desire to unite with his beloved.

Analogies help us express our ideas to people who haven't learned them by utilizing thoughts that are usually known by most of us and have parallels with our concepts that we would like to express. Consequently, in the communication-making use of analogies, you will find two common points.

One is the fact that suggestions used as analogies are usually known by many, and two of these suggestions used as analogies and the thought that we want to communicate making use of these analogies have common points or common traits.

Now the question you have to ask is: How can we make use of this idea of typical points for analyzing, innovating, and managing?

To analyze, control, and innovate making use of the typical points, we should find, refine, modify, and remove them. To do this, we should consult many questions. These questions could assist us in recognizing and perfecting them before we can alter, remove, or add new areas.

The aim is seeing the whole situation as being a pair of typical areas knit together and other areas.

Through the knowledge of the nature of these areas, we ought to be in a position to see the map of all the options, options of shift. There is a 7 step procedure as follow:

Step one: Identity: first question to ask: What are the typical points?

That identical, similar, between or saying in time times, people, spaces, things, ideas, and actions, etc.

Step two: Challenge:

1st question to ask:

Do we perceive a typical issue that doesn't occur?

Challenge your observation by asking: Is the fact that in reality so? What if it is not?

The second question to ask: Are there a few typical factors that we are ignorant of?

Step three: Refine: the first question to ask: Can there be any vagueness or ambiguity in the understanding of the typical point?

Remember, the instance of understanding is power. The term' power' was ambiguous. Each typical point should have a clear definition. There mustn't be any overlapping, fuzzy, not clear meanings.

2nd question to ask: Do we missing a little info about the same issue?

It is feasible that some typical areas are hidden deep inside apparent observations. You have to dig deep inside.

3rd question to ask: Do we mistake two and typical factors being one or overlapping?

For instance, etiquettes of the conference are typical things between individuals of a lifestyle. Etiquettes for conference close friends aren't like those for strangers. One could mistake the two etiquettes assuming that all things considered, both friends and strangers are people.

4th question to ask: Are the typical factors found instant on the areas between what they are typical?

For instance, let us view a, b, c, d, and e, and the c is roughly in the center of a, and e although not the typical between a, and e. In this particular situation, d, c, and b are jointly typical between and a, and e while b is typical between a, and c. C is typical between b and d and d among c and e.

The target must be to knit the whole picture with no missing piece of info, with no jump, and to go from one point to solely fast then one so that we can see all the possibilities.

Recall the earlier example of visiting the market of new fruit and choosing to travel to purchase medication. A jump out of fresh fruits to driving wouldn't justify how and why we instantly chose to go to a medication when we are buying new fruits.

Step four: Explain: the first question to ask: What are the dynamics of the typical areas?

Their definitions, limitations, functions, and causes of existence.

Step five: Knit the picture: 1st question to ask: What are additional factors between what they are typical?

The second question to ask: How can they connect with other factors between what they are typical?

Step six: Innovate and manage: the first question to ask: How could all of them be modified?

For instance, a typical wall exists between the office room and the library. I want to have fast access to a room that is next. I can change the wall and create a doorway.

Mental Models | 45

The second question to ask: How could there be a deliberate launch associated with a new frequent point?

For instance, there is no intercom between the room and another room where my father works. I could add an intercom that will be a typical thing for quick communication.

3rd question to ask: How could several typical points be stayed away from? Or could many of them be deleted from the device?

For instance, among the windows of my room opens towards a college. During the mid-day break, the children come to play and ground. This produces so much noise. And the window acts as the same thing for enabling this to come to my room.

The glass panels of the window weren't soundproof. What I did was buying new glass panes that had been good edits and shut the windows during the midday break. This particular way, I stay away from the typical point allowing for the noise available in my room when I have to.

Step seven: The fundamental picture: 1st Question to ask: What is the photograph of the whole situation with our knowledge of typical areas?

With this fundamental setup, you can find, assess, deal with, and innovate some circumstance, or fix the issue. You have discovered how the typical details could be used to develop and evaluate arguments, and how these points allow you to innovate, and control something in life.

This particular simple arrangement equips you with all you need to have for simplifying your life. Nevertheless, the necessary knowledge isn't enough for sensible affairs of life. The use of certain areas of life is required.

The same as the brain is the central process in our lives, and it is a typical thing in every exercise in our lives, economic activity influences our lives also. It engages in economic activity, whether it is not for profit business, labor supply, personal company, or investing.

The economic activity has an impact on the rest of the recreation of our lives. Thus, economic activity is yet another common point in our lives. Since it is central, it is between other actions; it consistently influences our life. For economic activity, the main role is of competition.

Whether it is NGO or any people, compete for with one another for there is an agreement. The understanding that money is vital for living, the money is central for our modern lives as we no longer stay in primitive communal tribes.

Consequently, competition is a very common thing since it is central in economic activity; it is in between most activities in industry, it consistently influences most choices, and it is the same in most kinds of activities. What this means is that among the important frequent stage of life is competitors.

Everybody faces competition in life. In life, either we battle, or we run permanently. If perhaps we run, we end up tired and unfulfilled. Thus, our only option is fighting, to struggle, and to compete.

But if we are not built with knowledge and tools of contests, we inevitably lose our precious time and scarce online resources. We drop competitions also. Hence, there is an importance to learn competition.

CHAPTER 5

The Art of Creative Thinking

Creative people are' unreasonable' since they defy the norm, and therefore are undaunted by the grotesque and the irregular.

They delight in dallying amorously with the abnormal, the unorthodox, and the unconventional. Every advance and every progress that humanity has thus far attained is because of the creative powers of outstanding minds.

One could master all the rules of the principles and rationale thinking of logic: it won't help. The quest for knowledge, the discovery of fact, and the wisdom of daily life, in reality, autumn incalculably outside the purchased world of logic and rationalism, for life is too fluent and insanely changeful interspersed with surprises and shocks. The puzzles of living can't regularly be cracked with stereotyped responses; they involve innovative evaluation.

Creativeness needs the courage to conceive thoughts and visualize functions outside the orbit of reason and the world of rationality. For popular language, it is known as' thinking outside of the box'!

That is what imagination is about: taking the untrodden path that nobody has had before! Creativeness will be the unfettering of intellectual imprisonment from the shackles of conservative and conventional dogmatism.

Unimaginable, it will be for anyone being inventive who locks himself in the chambers of dogmatic intellectualism and contents himself in the narrow borders of axiomatic theories. Innovative thinkers share sure attributes in common: they don't fear to step into new domains;

They unflappably flirt with not related fields of knowledge, and they enthusiastically undertake voyages into unfamiliar disciplines. If truth is uttered, imagination isn't for individuals that are impoverished in the pursuit of innovative thinking.

Many of us are held again in our assumption that imagination is usually about finding or inventing anything essentially new and novel, and consequently, it is a prerogative of a gifted several. What an unalloyed misconception!

For reality, imagination happens to be an aptitude to relate unrelated ideas in something exceptionally distinct imagination plants with the convergence of disparate ideas, thoughts, or concepts.

Linear thinking compared to intersectional thinking

Since proper training is created to perfect the basics of specialized disciplines, dutifully, it shapes the brain in the mold of linearity.

Simply put, linearity is one-dimensional thinking! It subjects the brain to inquire in the terminology of logical analysis and reasoning while depriving, at the same time, the ability to think outside of the beaten track. It, therefore, becomes a workout in mastering the mundane and the monotonous making predictable changes in the process.

Linear thinking is incapable of stirring extreme changes since it restricts the expanse circle inside THAT it conducts its adventure in learning. It dares not step from the group as it satiates itself with producing small upgrades here and changes that are minor there with little interruption to the status quo.

The majority of the new developments activated by linear thinking are of this particular kind: policy

Mental Models | 51

changes, procedure modifications, structural modifications fall into the linear class. These are not earth-shattering and life-changing transformations but incremental improvements.

Intersectional thinking, on the other hand, techniques in unpredictable directions that, as a result, can easily alter the context radically. Intersectional thinking uninhibitedly cuts through different fields, disciplines, domains, and areas to produce connections between apparently unrelated concepts and ideas; it makes cutting edge ideas and principles.

Examples in intersectional thinking abound: whether it is Steve Jobs making the appearance THAT he discovered through the program in calligraphy and incorporating that understanding to iMacs, iPods, iPads or iPhones;

Whether it is Alexander Graham Bell who had mixed the interests in auto mechanics, ventriloquism, speech therapy, and music to invent the telephone; or whether it is Leonardo da Vinci that drew his abundance of inspiration and knowledge from the different disciplines for example engineering, architecture, painting, sculpting, geology, and anatomy they virtually all point to the ability of these males to connect the unrelated into a distinctive effect.

As a rule, intersectional believing involves an open mind to link theories and concepts from one discipline with principles and theories in someone else.

No matter whether it is around food recipe, academic research, or telecom networks, linking unrelated ideas is anything of attractiveness in itself that lies in the center of imagination. Intersectional thinking is not difficult since its secret lies in the interlinking and interlocking of disparate suggestions and bringing about a synthesis.

Barriers to creative thinking creativity can't be purchased or faked; neither could it be learned from books though it may be created with a bit of adjustment of how we feel. The barriers to creativity live in the brain as conceptual blocks freezing the ability to conceive alternative ideas and solutions to constraints and problems.

At each moment, each individual is inundated with more huge sensations than we can perhaps manage. While you read this, you most likely are unaware of the existence of your eyes, the sounds in the feel, or the background of your clothes on your skin.

Although every one of this info is offered, you most likely weren't mindful of any of it until and unless you purposely paid attention to those feelings.

We naturally can't consider the infinite stream of stimuli fighting with each other to get our conscious attention. Doing this would subject us to info overload and drive us to madness.

Hence, we remove those stimuli that aren't appropriate and selectively deal with those that we consider helpful for your purpose. This particular selective attention, aside from its usefulness, censors essential and comfortable clues that most likely could have life-changing potential.

Right training has molded us to consider in the terminology of reason and logic. The infatuation with' right' solutions has always taken precedence over' imagination' while at the office.

The fetishism with the right method of doing things was provided value over' innovativeness.' This has resulted in the petering from improvisation and experimentation, killing imagination in the procedure.

Imagination typically suffers at the hands of four shortcomings: constancy, complacency, compression, and commitment.

Constancy: A universal concept is decreed upon us that constancy for thought, word, and deed is a virtue. Any unique low inconstancy is likely to be tagged as untrustworthy, undesirable, and unreliable.

In businesses, the main feature of command methods is to reduce deviation from the identified standard. Constancy, doubtless, is brought to some divine state in the daily scheme of things.

Nevertheless, upon closer scrutiny, the same constancy, that strives to take expected outcomes, stamps underfoot the speck of imagination fighting to unleash its creative expression.

A lot of people, when confronting an issue, contend with it depending on their past experiences or search for precedence in resolving it. They believe vertically! Not sideways!

A vertical concentration assumes a narrow gaze is defining the issue in one way instead of interpreting it in multiple ways. Any person possessed by a conviction that it is not worth looking at many options will continue to be undermined in creative thinking.

The bane of constancy arises in restricting oneself to subjecting an issue to individual interpretation.

A problem, as an example, is defined and evaluated in several interpretations: through symbolic or non-verbal interpretation, algebraically or numerically; by using sensory images for example smell, taste, sound, touch, seeing; via thoughts and emotions like excitement, anger, happiness, hatred; or utilizing obvious imagery like mental maps.

The greater diversified the interpretation of an issue. The greater would be the risks of developing innovative results.

Constancy is inimical to creativity. Constancy is only a procession of sameness and similarity

Commitment: Another virtue that appears as an obstacle to the imagination is commitment. It triggers the creative juices to freeze, particularly when we determine difficulties in the glow of previous encounters.

The overall human inclination is seeing the latest issues as variants of previous occurrences; thus, we create answers much like the people that have been effective in previous times, completely oblivious that issues are visible in new ways and interpreted differently. The resolve for history allows us to contend with issues stereotypically, not innovatively.

Dedication to a specific view could also prevent in seeing commonalities among various issues and coming one strategy that addresses several problems in the identical time.

Viewing disparate components holistically is a characteristic of innovative thinkers. Ray Kroc, the male behind the development of McDonald's, didn't invent fast food. He was a salesman before he connected various concepts into something different.

Linking a standardized menu, even food preparation techniques, consistent service quality, hygiene of amenities, affordable food production, and disposable diet substances, while combining them with his sales experience, entrepreneurial ambition, relationship building, negotiating talent, he demonstrated a distinctive method of imagination.

Not one single feature stated above is different, but he integrated them to create a concept that, to this particular day, remains a profitable and robust business model.

Compression: Too much info and redundant data are adequate to get anyone crazy., time pressure and resource scarcity constrain our ability to check out an issue extensively. In the process, we display out a lot of specifics. We impose synthetic constraints after ourselves when we cope with issues.

We sketch boundaries, sit within them, and conjure up solutions to our riddles. There is an aversion also because of impersonal influences or personal choice to brainstorm rightly in dealing with issues. Often, folks make assumptions without knowing them and exploring available alternatives to access concealed clues.

Compression depletes the ability to sort the wheat from the chaff and power to cull out incorrect, misleading, or information that is irrelevant. Indiscriminate minds incorporate a mishmash of data to a chaotic bundle and then be burdened by its weight. It increases the complexity of the issue while defying the ease of problem definition.

Complacency: translated, it is mental laziness! It arises out of insufficient aversion and curiosity for mental work. Unwillingness to ask questions, procrastination to study, and worry of the humiliation of exposing one's ignorance are many the reasons why individuals start to be less curious. two elements are essential here: one) an enthusiasm to ask questions and two) an eagerness to uncover solutions.

Overcome mental inertia! Imagination occurs if you try using the right side of your brain that is about intuition, synthesizing, and playfulness. Our extremely organized training and regimented work often lay focus on utilizing more of the left part of the human brain that is accountable for rational, sequential and analytical jobs, and seldom its counterpart sitting at the complete opposite conclusion.

Use each side of the mind to be creative. While the right hemisphere assists in germinating innovative concepts, its left counterpart complements by processing and interpreting them via logical analysis.

Competition today comes out of every nook, corner, and direction of the universe. The best competitive advantage is not in the income gap, entitlement gap, education gap, or abilities gap; it is based on the imagination gap. Creativity often will get to be the deciding factor between the have-nots and the haves of the contemporary world.

CHAPTER 6

Systems Thinking Basic Concept

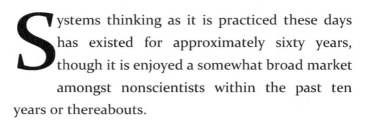

Systems thinking as it is practiced these days has existed for approximately sixty years, though it is enjoyed a somewhat broad market amongst nonscientists within the past ten years or thereabouts.

Systems thinking is a better way of taking a look at events, individuals, and entities in the world. It consists not of a pair of strict methodologies or theories, but only a set of principles and applications that collectively offer methods thinkers a new, likely more expansive view of the world.

In a sense, methods don't exist objectively in the world and instead rely upon human observer viewing processes or entities as systems. Nevertheless, viewing items on the world as methods could be an incredibly effective method of making sense of their behavior.

Systems thinkers tend to see the world as a set of recurring relationships, processes, and changes. In a feeling, systems' thinking is a beautiful and necessary opposite to the beneficial perspective that regular, reductionist science has.

Individuals who are self-described methods thinkers draw upon a vibrant literature foundation, both non-scientific and scientific. This base consists of methods theories, philosophies, and methodologies.

Systems thinking could be put on to nearly every location that we wish to learn better, which includes businesses, machines, social organizations, the human brain, and computer systems.

Allow me to share four standard methods principles that can provide you with a sense of what methods thinking is approximate.

Systems environment boundary: Seeing the many processes and entities on the world as methods needs, we draw a boundary between the device in question and its environment.

For instance, if we wish to see a family unit as being a method, the boundary we sketch could split the people of the household out of the schools, communities, and workplaces where they participate regularly.

If we wish to view a cell as being a method, the boundary may be the cell wall. Remember that the surroundings of a method might, when seen from another perspective, be other methods. Systems-environment boundaries might be sometimes conceptual or physical.

2. Open Versus Closed Methods: Some systems are relatively closed, meaning they minimize the quantity of influence that their environments have on the operations. More open systems, by comparison, may change significantly depending upon inputs from their environments.

For instance, a little organization is significantly really an open system than is a car engine: the business is changing to be able to survive, even though the motor essentially has to remain precisely the same if it is operating effectively.

3. Self-Contained: One characteristic of methods is the fact that many of the procedures and elements required for them to do their various functions are contained in the systems themselves.

Naturally, about all methods consume several inputs from the earth (or other means) then change those inputs into outputs. Nevertheless, wholesome methods can do their functions (based upon green

62 | William Bell

inputs and driving outputs to the environment) in a self-contained fashion.

4. Adaptive: Sure devices of higher complexity, like social systems and biological organisms, can adjust to ever-changing environmental conditions.

Simply put, whether or not the world changes over time (i.e., macro weather patterns, food types available, modifications in other community systems, etc.), they are usually capable of adapting, make it, and flourish within these new circumstances.

Though the area of methods thinking had not even hatched in time of the quote, it is apparent that Einstein knew about systems thinking, even if he did not call it that. He managed to understand that if we always approached difficulties, in the same way, we will continue to get the same results.

We, humans, are creatures of habit, and we quite often think it is hard to identify patterns of conduct that are counterproductive. Systems thinking provides programs and processes THAT enable organizations to see connections and patterns, leading to greater efficiency.

The discipline of methods thinking evolved from the area of systems dynamics, and it is both a pair of tools and a completely new means of thinking involving a new language. In systems thinking, we consider the whole system instead of attempting to break it d to its specific parts; that is, we start to be expansive in our thinking instead of reductive.

By taking a look at the whole, we are more effective at seeing patterns and interrelationships over time. We likewise start to comprehend the presenting issue might be symptomatic of deeper issues inside the device, and so we begin searching for the root causes. In doing this, we move from assigning focus and blame on the desired results.

Systems thinking is circular and proactive, instead of linear thinking, that is likely to be reactive. You will find three fundamental ideas of methods thinking: reinforcing feedback, balancing responses, and delays. Amplifying or reinforcing feedback loops are what fuel development or produce a decline of methods.

They often spiral up or d, though they hardly ever happen in isolation. There are limitations both to decline and growth. A basic illustration of a reinforcing loop is precisely how an organization's efficiency can affect development, which in turn, influences monetary incentives that will come full circle to impact efficiency. This particular loop can go either on the right path or a wrong path but eventually stops at an outer limit.

Balancing or stabilizing feedback loops are the ones that try to maintain equilibrium. These methods are goal-oriented and can do whatever is required to reach or maintain that objective. The preceding example of driving an automobile is a balancing loop since the aim is reaching the preferred location.

The driver will do what it takes to arrive at that destination efficiently and safely. In businesses, we are bumping up over a balancing loop when there are attempts to make the change take us to wherever we began.

We encounter resistance to change as the existing product is attempting to keep a specific goal. The goal, nonetheless, might not be visible; we might find we have to uncover the mental types that are keeping that process installed before we have some hope of changing it.

Delays are unavoidable in any program but are usually not recognized. Delays trigger instability of methods, and intense action to compensate for delays will result in businesses to undershoot or overshoot.

What Are the Characteristics of Methods Thinkers?

A systems thinker is but one who:

Sees the whole picture.

Modifications perspectives to notice new leverage areas in complex systems.

Looks for interdependencies.

It explains how mental models create our futures.

Pays attention to the long term.

"Goes wide" to consider the complicated effect and causal relationships.

Finds in that unanticipated effects emerge.

Reduces the "water line" to concentrate on structure, not blame.

Holds the tension of controversy and paradox without attempting to resolve it efficiently.

Systems thinkers are people who think outside of the box. They know that you'll find no right answers, different paths to similar results. They recognize that quick fixes will likely lead right back to anywhere they started from and therefore develop patience with the concept that cause and effect aren't strongly related in space and time.

They realize that things may get even worse before they get better, though they have learned to take the very long view. In doing this, they can tap the innovative synergy that exists within organizations.

How Can Organizations Use Systems Think?

Like the prior four disciplines, there are some methods to use systems thinking inside a company, and every organization should discover what fits perfectly in the organizational culture. Nevertheless, you can find crucial parts of systems thinking considering.

Below is one possible strategy that includes these essential parts:

Events: Begin the process of methods thinking by telling the story of the present situation. It is crucial to hear as many perspectives as you can. Nevertheless, do not jump to solutions quickly. It could be required to make a fast solution but do this with the understanding that it is a measure that is not created for a very long-term solution. Meanwhile, exploring the dynamics of the event or issue in much detail.

Behavioral patterns: Track the circumstance with a length of time. Search for patterns and trends that go below the surface area. Go again in history, if you have received the information. Those patterns are crucial indicators for the product.

Systemic structure: Discover interrelationships in the trends and patterns you have found. Search for balancing and reinforcing feedback and determine delays in the product. Uncover the mental models that drive these patterns.

Mental models: Create innovative mental versions to introduce change to the device. Be patient - but there will be delays, and things could get even worse before they get better. Track and assess the consequences of the changes. Determine if there exist unintended consequences and determine what requires tweaking.

Even though this may seem like a relatively straightforward procedure, it is much from it. You will find challenges that are many to using systems thinking, the largest of that is traditions and habits.

Patterns of behavior are tough to identify and more stringent to change, and we quite often feel pressure to act rapidly with little or no systemic info. To discover the balance between taking care of the present and producing the future is never simple.

What Are the Advantages of Systems Thinking?

Systems' believing could be the thread that ties the four disciplines of organizational learning. Most organizations engaging in methods thinking are competent to:

Develop new means of looking at old issues.

Integrate new information more readily.

See interrelationships and effect and cause more obviously.

Develop patience with implementing shift and tolerating delays.

Step far from the blame game toward shared responsibility.

Considered the entire concept instead of the parts.

Even though every one of the advantages mentioned above can have an inordinate length of time to understand, the expenditure in building methods thinkers is well worth the effort and time. Ultimately, groups practicing methods thinking will be ready to step up to that subsequent level of contemplating to resolve problems and make their ideal futures.

They will have higher command over their destiny and be a little more nimble in answering environmental improvements. What an eco-friendly way to remain one step in front of the competition?

And the standard systems thinking concepts, below are five more critical concepts.

1. **Goal Seeking:** All devices continuously attempt to achieve one or more goals. An engine creates horsepower to do work. A cell reproduces and sometimes serves other cells in particular ways. A human being seeks to keep living and to recreate (among some other goals).

A business may be trying to make an income or benefit people, method objectives will never be attained entirely in a static sense but are preferably continuously being concurrently attained and sought after by the device.

2. **Differentiation:** Systems are comprised of many parts. In a design of business that has a unique part to play in the context of the complete program.

3. **Interdependence:** The differentiated system elements are interdependent. That is, every one of the parts should operate in conjunction with the other

70 | William Bell

parts in the device to be able to further the objectives of the device.

4. **Feedback:** Systems are continuously checking inputs from the environment; inputs can take the type of info, power, or several other information.

As the inputs change on quantity or form through time, the device responds to those modifications by adjusting its internal processes so that its goals can continue to be met. This procedure for making adaptive changes in reaction to changing inputs is known as negative feedback.

5. **Regulation:** Feedback is an excellent method in which a method self regulates. This regulation process is the thing that allows systems to adjust to their environments. Methods are usually exchanging outputs and inputs with their environments; therefore, regulation is a better way of mediating between the constantly changing atmosphere and the devices' internal parts.

CHAPTER 7

Critical Thinking Concept

———◯·◯———

Critical thinking is a phrase that has turned out to be the most recent buzz word. In previewing the American Heritage Dictionary definition of 'think,' one finds an extensive in-depth description one that contains the meaning of' critical thinking.'

From my knowledge of the term 'think'it suggests using self-discipline to concentrate on a specific subject; to actively and effectively process; masterfully conceptualize, generate understanding, analyze, synthesize or assess all info gathered; think about the source; view, reason, reflect, experience, communicate.

From its most exemplary construct, the word 'think' is dependent on intellectual values that transcend subject material divisions: clarity, breadth, depth, good reasons, sound evidence, relevance, consistency, precision, accuracy, and fairness that are integrated into the' thinking' procedure.

To fully complete the' thinking' procedure on every subject entails the evaluation of all

- ○ The precepts, notions, and the exact elements or structures of believed implicit in most reasoning:
- ○ Objective, issue or question-at-issue;
- ○ Assumptions, concepts;
- ○ Empirical grounding;
- ○ Reasoning from top to conclusions;
- ○ Consequences and implications;
- ○ Objections from other viewpoints; and
- ○ Frame of reference.

Utilizing thinking to the fullest extenta.k.a.' critical thinking, one has to be responsive to the adjustable subject matter, problems, and purposes incorporating everything in an interwoven method, including

- ○ logical thinking,
- ○ moral thinking,
- ○ economic thinking,
- ○ anthropological thinking,
- ○ historical thinking,
- ○ mathematical thinking,
- ○ philosophical thinking, and
- ○ ethical thinking.

Thinking has two components:

1. A framework of info and idea processing and generating abilities,
2. The pattern, dependent on intellectual commitment, of utilizing all abilities to guide actions.

It is contrasted with:

1. The simple acquisition and retention of info by yourself, since it entails a specific way where info is wanted and treated;
2. The simple possession of abilities, since it entails the continuous use of them; and
3. The simple utilization of those abilities ("as an exercise") with no acceptance of their results.

Thinking varies based on the motivation underlying it and the habits or indoctrination since childhood. When seated in selfish motives, it is commonly manifested in the competent manipulation of suggestions in service of one's, or one's groups', vested interest.

As a result, it is usually intellectually flawed, however pragmatically profitable it may be. When seated in intellectual integrity and fair-mindedness, it is generally of a more significant order intellectually, although governed by the cost of "idealism" by all habituated to its selfish use.

Thinking is different from any individual; attacks of irrational or undisciplined thought govern everybody. Thinking quality is usually a situation of degree and determined by, and other things, the quality, and level of expertise of a particular domain of thinking and about a specific category of concerns.

Nobody is an entirely more profound thinker through-and-through, but to a degree, blind spots, with various insights, subject to different tendencies towards self-delusion. Because of this, the improvement of thinking skills and dispositions is a lifelong endeavor.

Albeit primitive thinking starts in utero, it is not until a kid begins to discuss is it mostly accepted that the individual has cognition. This is tragically restricting to the child's knowledge of confirming their ability to believe and reason.

Regrettably, the moment the kid starts to verbalize their ability of complete thinking they are told such items as:' Children are being noticed and never heard '--albeit that stage has to some amount start to be out, though the idea continues to be conveyed in some ways--'Because, I stated so." Don't communicate back.'

This eventual prohibition to' in-depth thinking' is often accompanied by a smack/slap for being disrespectful or sassy. My mother's preferred term to' shut me up' when she did not wish to pick up what I knew or wanted her to appear at was, "Now, Dorothy, do not be carried away." Thus, light believing is established.

We, then, arrive into adulthood, couching the thinking to ensure we do not offend or get reprimanded for saying something undesirable towards the person(s) engaged.

Not surprising then, the most significant deterrent to working out the complete spectrum of' thinking' or' critical thinking' will be the anxiety about showing up dumb when asking questions to be able to complete the in-depth' thinking' procedure fully.

People who did not encounter or were not deterred by these parental prohibitions produce sundry and various ways to compensate for others' trained shallow communication styles such as coining phrases and buzz words brainstorm, think tank, critical thinking, etc.

While these coined phases/buzz words work the purpose, it is a new rap for a birthright that had been unknowingly usurped.

Thinking is one thing we all inherently do. Differences in our thinking apt emanate from our biases and distorted views. Our biases and distorted views may stem from assumptions we have made or info provided to us we accepted as real.

To question our assumptions and the info provided to us will help us conduct evaluations that may nurture our ability to get value from our thinking. Since the result of our thinking dictate how

profitable we will be, cultivating our ability to believe (i.e., our ability to think critically) is essential.

Thinking critically is a complex process used to increase understanding, acquire understanding, and resolve issues. The critical attitude calls for keeping an open mind while gathering and interpreting information to understand a couple of likely answers to raised questions.

The task needs that each possible solution is extensively examined for the likelihood of accuracy. The critical thinking process finishes with the choosing of the solution that contains the highest chance of accuracy.

Critical thinking has been identified in many ways. Some people think thinking critically is a higher-order thinking ability that involves evaluating arguments and generating judgments that may result in the improvement of beliefs.

Others think critical thinking consists of determining and analyzing arguments using reasoning abilities. Both sights include examining arguments.

Arguments should be analyzed to decide whether the info fulfills the Universal Intellectual Standards. The Universal Intellectual Standards try the quality of info. The Universal Intellectual Standards idea encourages critical thinking.

The Universal Intellectual Standards assess:

* The transparency of information seeks elaboration

* The reliability of information seeks verification

* The accuracy of information seeks specifics

* The importance of information seeks a connection

* The depth of information seeks factor for complexities

* The breath of information seeks additional viewpoints

* The reasoning of information seeks consistency

* The significance of information seeks importance

* The fairness of information seeks neutrality

Other concepts have surfaced to clarify the abilities involved in critical thinking. One idea entails

Interpretation (categorization, decoding significance, and clarifying meaning);

Analysis (examining suggestions, identifying arguments, and examining arguments); evaluation (assessing statements and assessing arguments);

Inference (querying proof, conjecturing options, and drawing conclusions);

Explanation (stating outcomes, justifying methods, and showing arguments);

Self-regulation (self-correction and self-examination); and

Deduction (analogical thought, utilizing analogies, formulating hypotheses, the extension of debates, ability to develop expertise, prediction, modeling, and adaptive reasoning).

While these principles could describe the abilities involved in thinking critically, the critical attitude could be more plainly defined.

Critical thinking begins with a hunt for a solution to a question. About the most basic methods employed in critical thinking is asking probing questions. Whereas the uncritical thinker may accept the original answer given, the crucial thinker will challenge all answers.

Critical thinkers, while seeking/challenging answers, should be ready to keep control of their mental activities. Critical thinkers must use their minds to make sense of their world by carefully examining their thinking and the thinking of others to be able to enhance understanding.

The crucial thinker must have the ability to track inconsistencies within his/her, and others' reasoning. Checking out one is personal thinking for inconsistencies assists explicit biases and distorted perspectives and results in invaluable critical thinking that nurtures success.

The Real Difference Between Critical Thinking and Skeptical Thinking

Many would state the critical thinking abilities are far better compared to user-friendly thinking abilities, though I disagree, in many regards, they are two ways that are different at attacking the same issue, and sometimes getting to the same solution.

Having a skeptical mind likewise helps since it is you questioning the premises before you begin. The truth is you need to question all that you see, wherever you go, and you should not hesitate to make judgments about everything you observe, see, feel, and expertise.

If you are throwing out all the observations in the industry for everything you call critical thinking, you can end up in under a beneficial circumstance.

Since you used logic and crucial processes in coming to an answer, or the following step in a multilayered problem or challenge doesn't mean you should not be suspicious of every sub-component across the way, including your starting point.

I look for individuals that are utilizing innovative critical thinking abilities too often are over self-confident with the conclusion they have created, nearly to the stage that they won't work with their critical thinking abilities to question their data points and the foundation of their argument.

I would state in the event that you would like to be a great decision-maker, you must always keep a suspicious brain, use critical thinking abilities often and early, and trust your gut when something does not really feel appropriate to return and examine the parts of your answer, together with the givens, theories, or areas of contention you began with.

Finally, do not let an academic who promises to have or have the appropriate answer demand that they are correct, when they base that conclusion on the reality they use critical thinking abilities in the procedure.

The viewpoint of what reason is, what it does, and what it is effective at was over-embellished for decades, if not thousands of years. Surely I am hoping you'll please think about everything and think about it; therefore, you create the best choices in your life, company, or any capacity that you are helping.

Stages of Thinking Critically

Bertrand Russell said: "To be in a position to focus for a significant time is crucial to hard achievement." In both our personal life and career, there are lots of conditions that need people to think critically.

This consists of conditions like working with a crisis, a complaint out of a buyer, determining whom to market and buying expensive equipment. The list is unquestionably not exhaustive.

Compared with innovative thinking that expects you to believe from the box sometimes and arrives at the most ludicrous suggestions, critical thinking on the flip side involves a regular practice of evaluation of facts, assumptions, and data to be able to reach a logical conclusion.

This provides the suggestion that critical thinking is fairly a lot more boring compared to innovative thinking that doesn't discount for coming with crazy flamboyant concepts and ideas.

However, critical thinking doesn't need to be boring, and it may be as good if not more than creative thinking if you learn the fine art of having the ability to use the procedure of critical thinking.

Fundamentally critical thinking consists of the conscientious program of the 5 stage process. By using this 5 stage system, you will notice you start to be great and solving those issues that might have long-reaching implications and making efficient choices that leave no room for regret later on.

Allow Me to Share the Five Stages:

Stage 1: Identify the primary key issue that has to be solved. It is a fact that during discussions and meetings, there is an inclination that people get diverted on the primary key parts of what they want to resolve.

To become a highly effective critical thinker, you should initially begin by identifying the primary key issue in the issue or situation you need to deal with and resolve. Please create this particular view it occasionally to ensure you are conscious you are not getting sidetracked and going on a wild goose chase.

Stage 2: Gather related data and facts Critical thinking is helpful in situations such as combating customer complaints or making an inquiry into a thing that has occurred and of a situation like preparing a big conference or function when nothing could be left to chance. In these situations, you must gather all the pertinent data and facts so you can work towards a good outcome.

Stage 3: Clarify feasible assumptions, concepts, and theories. Likely, you might not have all the appropriate data and facts. This is particularly so if you are getting is a new task, and thus there are no previous experiences to work with. Below you have to take a look at possible assumptions, theories, and concepts pertaining to your situation.

This will involve postulating a worst case and best case scenario in addition to thinking with the system that may be put in place when all these were to occur. Occasionally this is called deliberate thinking that is a lot a subcategory of critical thinking.

Stage 4: Look for Evidence to allow for your cause of action

Critical thinking most will involve you need to produce an informed choice. This then would entice the interest detractors who would have their hidden agenda to attack or criticize your decision. Whatever you have to accomplish is having tough evidence that supports your cause of action and be in a position to provide a strong case in your favor.

Stage 5: Check and hold in view any inconsistencies

There is no such thing as a right choice or an ideal strategy for a crucial issue. What you might have attained is coming up with a good solution that could or might not resolve a significant component of the issue or a pragmatic choice that handles the situation at hand. It is thus vital that you confirm and retain in view any inconsistencies that may develop in these circumstances.

Inconsistencies below relate to those concerns that may have more than one possible answer or doesn't always apply to all. It might not be feasible so that you can solve these inconsistencies in the present time though it will be wise to remember this to ensure you might focus on it later to try and solve it if this may be possible at all.

Adding these 5 phase procedures will pave the way for you to be a highly effective crucial thinker and therefore causing you to an advantage in your organization in addition to enabling you to create an unbiased view of life.

Let us see whether critical thinking can help.

A rightly cultivated vital thinker does four particular things. We will take each subsequently to considered if it leads us to our two questions.

1. "Raises essential questions and problems, formulating them obviously and precisely."

What important questions will we ask ourselves? How about:

"What do we have to express in words that we can't express in another way (such as via nonverbal, physical demonstrations, sounds, or pointing at something)?" or

"What words are most crucial in our everyday lives?"

Alright, we have our questions. So now we require guidance on how to reply to them.

2. "Gathers and assesses irrelevant information, utilizing abstract concepts to interpret it rightly, coming to well-reasoned conclusions and answers, testing them against pertinent criteria and standards."

What "relevant information" do we have? Effectively, we understand that words are usually classified in a minimum of two usual ways:

a. Words could be nouns, pronouns, verbs, adverbs, adjectives, and prepositions. [This is not especially beneficial, is it?]

b. Words could be categorized by topic, like communication, employment, emotions, and then family. [This seems a lot more promising.]

What "abstract ideas" could we use to interpret word-groups?

Existence, survival, and relationships are rather abstract.

If perhaps we use existence in the abstract to understand our word categories, our solutions" and "conclusions could be the two terms must be direct regarding existing as a man is.

What "relevant standards" and criteria can we use testing that conclusion?

If the standard is the fact that you will find twenty terms to help us are living in that world, then terms associated with human existence seem sensible.

3. "Thinks open-mindedly inside alternate systems of consideration, assessing and recognizing, as need be, implications, their assumptions, and pragmatic consequences."

What assumptions could we have that would affect our choice of words?

We will have assumptions concerning what existence implies and, so, what we'd have to dwell in our world.

For instance, presence to some may imply survival, while to others, it may imply thriving and succeeding.

Even if we determine presence as survival, we might still have distinct assumptions about what we have to live. Some may say we require food, clothing, and shelter, while others may say we'd like norms, community, and language to live by.

Each assumption has clear implications, every one of that can't be tackled in twoo terms.

Critical thinking has simultaneously widened our understanding of and complexity regarding the first issue.

4. "Communicates rightly with other people in determining solutions to complicated problems."

At this stage, you can consider how crucial it would be discussing these assumptions and conclusions with other people. We wouldn't be living by yourself in our world of twenty words.

When Tina used this as an exercise, the groups could figure out their words in ten minutes. We want the culture of others to do the job this through.

Would you begin figuring out these two important words to live by?

What criteria would you make use of?

Colors of Questioning That Sharpen Critical Thinking Skills

Informational gathering procedures are created to help leaders in asking questions that facilitate the thinking abilities of recall and observation. Both recall and observation thinking skills are foundational to the collection and retention of certain information.

When wondering about advertising critical and creative thinking, it is essential to work with employees' responses to direct the following thoughts within dialogues and discussions. Be sure to make use of predetermined formulated thoughts for dictating, directing, or channeling employee responses.

Clues for posing effective and appropriate processing and probing questions are being discovered in the responses provided to the primary concerns that have been directed. Due to this particular, leaders need to be adept listeners to be able to question right processing concerns that provide about quality responses.

You will find seven distinct kinds of processing questions that may be used to generate higher degrees of thinking. It is vital to understand when and where to use each:

Refocusing Questions

Refocus questions are essential whether employees aren't doing plenty of in-depth thinking or when they are talking about the topic. To refocus employee responses, executives might have to reacquaint them with that which was said, after that restate the core issue. It is essential to provide positive examples when refocusing workers back onto a specific subject, concept, or idea.

Clarifying Questions

Clarification is required whether responses are not transparent or if the leader thinks that better words might be used to express the responder's comment, idea, or opinion. Applying clarifying questions is an excellent method to build vocabulary.

Suitable clarification questions assist employees in explaining words and carrying meaning to their ideas. Many miscommunication and misunderstanding are induced by not clarifying words, feelings, ideas, or concepts appropriately and accurately.

Confirming Questions

Verifying questions offer opportunities to cite or give evidence for specific information or ideas. Responses tend to be based on individual experiences. When verifying information, it is essential to state what authorities or experts say is correct, and then to use a concept or generalization to allow for the information.

Redirecting Questions

Redirecting questions are intended to enhance private interactions. They need to be asked as often as you can within topical discussions and investigative meetings, sessions, or gatherings.

Redirecting questions gain a range of responses from many employees. Two ways to redirect thinking of food are asking: "What is an additional (way... thing... concept) we can provide to light to go over regarding this?" And, "Will another person provides another notion or insight on this particular topic?"

To Narrow the Focus Questions

Narrow the focus questions are used-to restrict the information of what is reviewed or discussed. They are based upon the "content characteristics" or the principles or strategies the leader plans to tackle, issue, and discuss.

Supporting Questions

Supporting questions must be asked to mentally link relationships between or among statements and evidence of inference, like cause/effect and prediction. Supporting thoughts offer opportunities to state factors for groupings, classifications, sequences, and labels.

Recall and Verification Questions

Verification is particularly crucial in recalling pieces of information, concepts, or information. Verification is gathered equally included in the main thing discussed, and beyond it, in the type of past experiences, authorities, generalizations, and principles.

Verifying through experiences, authorities, generalizations, and principles even further extend an employee's investigative skills by generating additional evidence to support facts.

When discussing certain facts of a specific idea or principle, the leader must ask few kinds of verifying thoughts to ensure that workers be enlightened by their understanding of the facts.

For instance, if a worker requested a basic verification query, "How do you manage to understand _____?" and the worker replies, "Because I _____." it is essential to follow up with another verification question that asks, "Where did you discover that information?"

Informational Gathering Processes

By providing personnel the chance to perform observing and recalling, they'll better understand the thinking abilities and turn into more conscious of the kinds of questions they have to question themselves when encountering circumstances that involve gathering and keeping info. Situations that require the observing thinking skill has to be representational and real.

While situations that call for the recalling thought ability must include thoughts with cue words recollection, this at first might seem unimportant or unnecessary, nonetheless, by utilizing cueing words, the leader helps personnel in understanding the way they gathered the topical information.

It allows employees to offer sound, verifiable evidence. For instance, if a leader says: "Tell me about the job process you did yesterday," personnel can say the way they felt about it, or discuss various assignments or tasks they liked.

By utilizing the "cues" for recall, "What do you remember about your last assignment in terminology importance?" the employee is more likely to talk straight to the specifics of the project or related responsibilities.

Use a Questioning Reflection Guide

There might come a moment every time a leader discovers that issues have surfaced when conducting a sure instructional session or meeting conversation with their employees.

It might be an excellent policy to tape and transcribe a minimum of a five or ten-minute active question and answer procedure. Then have another leader or peer critique the consultation and recommend ways to improve upon the issue and answer procedure.

Specific items to listen for are the forms of sequence and questions of questions that market employee responses and thinking, and how to better use the responses. Another essential thing to tune in for stands out as the pauses that arise throughout the "wait time" and the quantity of time that passes between responses and questions.

CHAPTER 8

How Important
Is critical Thinking?

———⊸⊶·⊷⊶———

C ritical thinking is checking out each side of a problem and then about your role based on factual proof you have gathered on the subject matter.

What is prior (background) understanding?

Previous knowledge is info you know about any subject before learning a more challenging concept. For example, you have to understand the solution to two plus two before you discover two by two.

You may hear serious thinking being described as better order thinking. The two phrases are interchangeable. These thinking abilities need anyone to draw inferences from the info they have been provided. The individual should also use deductive abilities from all the gathered information to make an informative choice or to have a position on the topic.

An individual who is enthusiastic about history will think differently from somebody who takes science more really. Consequently, the sayings, "Think like a historian," or "he is thinking like a scientist."

Companies demanded that critical thinking abilities be taught. The capacity to think critically depends upon the person's background knowledge of the topic. Also, he stated that situations ordinarily have a deeper structure compared to what many people see.

A treasure hunter will enjoy a cave up on a hill close to a beach. He suspected there could be lots of paths within the cave, so he was worried he could easily get lost.

He didn't possess a chart of the cave; all he had with him were several typical products like a bag and a flashlight. What might he do to make sure he didn't get lost attempting to get back from the cave later?

Willingham says the prior information of the story of Gretel and Hansel gave the pupils the thought of making some trail type. The ones that did not understand the story didn't recommend leaving a trail of sand.

The full understanding was being ready to connect what Gretel and Hansel did to what this particular treasure hunter must do, and in other words seeing that Hansel and Gretel's predicament was the like this particular treasure hunter's issue.

Dr. Willingham also Offers this to Say:

Individuals who wanted to teach critical thinking do assume that it is a skill, just like using a bicycle, and that, including other abilities, when you discover it, you can put it to use in every circumstance. Exploration from cognitive science suggests that believing isn't that kind of ability.

The tasks of contemplating are intertwined with the information of consideration (that is, domain knowledge). Hence, if you remind a pupil to "look at a problem from several perspectives," usually enough, he will learn that he should do so, but if he does not understand a lot about a problem, he cannot think of it from several perspectives.

You can instruct pupils' maxims (a short statement of useful principle) about precisely how they ought to believe. Still, with no background knowledge and training, they won't have the ability to apply the recommendations they memorize.

According to scientists, the handful of scientific studies that were performed regarding the usefulness of teaching critical thinking abilities demonstrate that these programs required time and effort and created modest advantages.

Critical thinking abilities are going to be nearly as good as the person's prior (background) understanding and nearly as good as the instructor.

Thus should critical thinking abilities be taught?

Math concepts will not do the job when a pupil knows what caused WWII and how it might have been stopped. There is not one set of critical thinking abilities that will change to other topics. Nevertheless, with this said, there are methods we can assist pupils in the beginning, imagining a lot more significantly.

Critical thinking methods (reasoning, problem making, and solving decisions or judgments) should not be taught individually but must be an all-natural addition to the curriculum.

The critical thinking strategies that pupils considered will be nearly as good as their teacher. One of the ways you can do this is by utilizing puzzles and reading mysteries. Asking pupils probing questions is yet another way to allow them to gain serious thinking strategies.

Including serious thinking techniques for each topic is extremely time-intensive since each topic has its set of concerns that will promote critical thinking. While incorporating these abilities every day into each topic, teaching info that pupils will have to acquire additional information cannot be excluded.

Something I believe is crucial to remember is the fact that all people come from various backgrounds. We are all affected by behavior about us. We are affected by:

Our ethnic group,

Our philosophy of life,

Religious beliefs,

Socioeconomic status,

Family history,

Our personality,

O intellect and how we put it to use, and

Our work ethic.

Every teacher might teach these essential critical thinking abilities, but since each one of us is affected by a wide variety of variables, not everybody will master these skills the same way or apply them into their life.

To have a happy marriage between critical thinking abilities and teaching, understanding is within the best interest of the student's academic achievement.

CHAPTER 9

Critical Thinking -
Things to Stay Away from Doing

———————$\infty\cdot\infty$———————

We can all figure out how to think more efficiently. The majority of the time, we get some things wrong about with no thinking that seems an unusual thing to say. Nevertheless, we do make fundamental mistakes in thinking and allow me to share many of the things we do.

This particular list is very long to recall, but if you identify many of your faults, you will do very well to create a smaller, more customer list. After that, don't forget the points on it, then be careful to stay away from them. Being conscious of any sloppiness inside your thinking is halfway to staying away from them.

Jumping to Conclusions

In our rush to conclude what we considered, we quite often miss out on essential steps; this is named leaping to conclusions. It is a thing we all do; often, we escape with it, and quite often, we do not. Jumping

Mental Models | 103

to conclusions in work that is written usually is readily spotted, although it can often take an additional reader to see the blunders we have created.

Neglecting to Believe Through Implications

Every choice we make, every road we take in our thought processes, has implications that could not always be evident. It is thus essential to consider anything through, as we say, to stay away from surprises later on.

To Lose an Eye on Our Objective

Losing an eye on what we wish to accomplish is a typical fault in thinking; we could easily get sidetracked by something that we get especially fascinating, or we may forget about where we are living. Writing stated goals is an excellent method of staying away from losing sight of an objective.

Being impractical Keeping to the plausible and the possible is essential, but using your imagination to think of other changes shouldn't stay away from since it occasionally yields unrealistic notions.

Concentrating on the trivial Ignoring what is vital and focusing on what may turn out to be unimportant or trivial may often occur. It is occasionally best that you step back from a problem to get some perspective.

Failing to discover contradictions If we spend effort and time in our thinking, it is clear that we fail to recognize things that cancel one another out.

Accepting Inaccurate Information

The problem with information is that it is occasionally wrong, but sounds perfect. To check things away is a great method of staying away from accepting info at face value without checking it. Ever taking things casual will be the next way forward.

To Ask Very Vague Questions

The wording of the questions you ask is vital, both to yourself and to all you ask. If you are formulating questions to question when reading, be cautious about altering them when additional info demands you to change course.

Giving Very Vague Answers

Being vague is often used to avoid particular issues. Performing this in writing is quickly seen by others, and you need to beware of performing it yourself. Rereading one thing you have written will help you to notice one thing that is excessively vague before an additional reader notices it.

Asking Packed Thoughts

The responses you receive rely on the questions you ask. Asking loaded questions suggests seeking out answers you wish to hear slightly compared to truthful ones. The questions you ask could indicate your prejudices.

Asking Irrelevant Issues

Similarly, asking questions with little bearing on the points that matter is also useless. Ask pertinent questions, and you will get answers you can work with, and that forces your thoughts forward.

Confusing Thoughts of Various Forms

Some questions generate Yes/No responses, while others generate useful answers. If your questions are stated clearly, your answers definitely will also be clear.

Providing Answers to Questions, We Are not Skilled in Answering.

Realizing the boundaries of our knowledge is a useful item to have the ability to do, and the willingness to acknowledge it is also precious. Do not stretch the credibility of your work by utilizing the info in tactics that are not reasonable or direct from the quality of info you are using.

Coming to Conclusions Based Upon Irrelevant or Inaccurate Info

One other way of thinking the same thing as the prior issue is you should not get started with stances or positions in arguments that are not supported by relevant and accurate info. Doing this would make the argument crumble under scrutiny.

Disregarding Info that Doesn't Support Our View

Only working with info that supports your views is equal to currently being partial, even though remaining incredibly appealing, ought to stay away from at all costs; be honest and dare to face your bias.

Making Inferences not Backed by Our Experience

Similarly, inferring items that aren't supported, either by evidence or experience or both, are irrational and can distort other statements in your work.

Distorting information and express it inaccurately It goes without saying that an individual should not alter information or alter it in every manner. To do so is risking making your whole argument when it has been determined the data you used was changed.

There seemed to be a really popular case recently of a learned specialist of genetics changing the information to fit his desired outcome. He was found out and did irreparable damage to his reputation.

Failing to note the inferences we do make Inferring isn't the same as proving. It is using the information to make suppositions, but these ought to be dependent upon reason and be capable and open entirely of getting discussed rationally.

Arriving at Unreasonable Conclusions

Arriving at conclusions that aren't affordable - based upon cause - is sure to create your entire work indefensible and insupportable.

Failure to Observe Your Assumptions

The assumptions - the items you are taking as a given, nearly - can stand as many as questioning. Poor awareness about making assumptions is a significant error and should be stayed away from.

The method to do this is asking yourself why you believe everything you do. If the causes aren't based upon clear evidence, you need to re-examine your thinking.

Making Unified Assumptions

While making assumptions is something that all of us do, the people we produce should be completely sensible and ready to accept scrutiny and observation. Assumptions that are not based upon open and rational factors are bias or, worse, prejudice.

Missing Key Ideas

Using all the information at your disposal, all that is relevant is essential. Lacking out crucial suggestions implies that your points are invalid and as such useless.

Utilizing Irrelevant Ideas

Again using whatever that is irrelevant is futile. The trouble is determining what is appropriate and what is not; relevant ideas will help to further your arguments, irrelevant suggestions will surely confuse, distort, and mask rational development in an argument.

Forming Confused Thoughts

Ideas that are confused are usually more effortlessly recognized by voicing them to others. Receptive listeners will often get on suggestions that are confused or unclear.

Forming Shallow Ideas

Concepts that don't stand up to rational scrutiny are even worse than useless; they can confound your thinking. Once again, voicing suggestions can help to stop all that do not' hold water,' as we say.

Misusing Text

In academic writing, making use of the right words is vital; utilizing terms with a lot a good impact on meaning to sandals that fit the context means that your writing is misinterpreted, that will imply you won't get recognition for it, although you understand in your mind what you mean. The capacity to express yourself concisely and precisely is everything.

Ignoring Related Viewpoints

In our drive to confirm the effort we have set out to create, we can often overlook viewpoints that, while going against our own, are useful and valid nevertheless to us.

Being open-minded is the means to stay away from disregarding opinions that might assist in making an argument better.

Not seeing problems from points of view apart from our Egocentric thinking leads us to arrive at conclusions that are insupportable, or worse, help make us appear self-centered and foolish.

To Be Ignorant of Our Prejudices

Confronting our prejudices are only able to occur when we are mindful of their existence, and since many our prejudices are essential to our sense of worth, who we are and the way we see ourselves, starting to be conscious of them may be painful. Nevertheless, most prejudice is damaging to a wholesome, healthy point of view.

CHAPTER 10

Positive Thinking

The biggest problem that stops lots of people from progressing by trouble is the reality that they get stalled in the detail of the problem. By concentrating on the particular issue, they are not allowing their subconscious mind to seek and offer the solution to the problem itself. This leads to you to be inert with the stress and the worry.

The day-to-day issues that are bothering you are not large enough to trouble your unconscious mind because they don't put your life in immediate danger.

Of the course of time, constant stress and pressure could detrimentally impact your health, and your unconscious mind would kick in at point by inducing your pain; therefore, you need medical assistance. Your day-to-day issues will not elicit assistance form your unconscious mind unless you expressly ask it for assistance.

Let us make use of the typical example of income worries. A lot of us, such as myself, have had times of financial strain, and there is little doubt that lots of more are likely to go through over the coming weeks when the financial meltdown will continue to attack the Western World.

The typical individual will care about the way to spend the mortgage or rent, the costs, and how you can put food on the kitchen table. Will they pay for to continue to operate the automobile? Oh, but they have to hold the automobile on the highway since they require the automobile to get to do the job.

Will they pay for the holiday that they guaranteed the kids. Christmas is nearby. Family birthdays are coming up. Wedding and Christening gifts have to be bought. The kids require new school and shoe uniforms and on and on and on.

Constant concentrate on the following paycheque and the number of times between pay cheques and what else could you give up for getting you through on the paycheque after. How are you going to spend the credit cards and the loans? Precisely what can you do to stop the bank charges when your payments bounce?

And then we have the regular concept, "How am I going to escape debt?" Meanwhile, your unconscious mind, your extremely effective subconscious brain, is perched there ticking along. In the short term, your debt won't kill you.

You have not asked your unconscious mind for assistance so that it only keeps on pumping the bloodstream and executing myriad other chemical responses it is to observe and control so you can stay in existence. It is happy doing its job, whistling on the project, while you are stressed on the nerve endings. You are living, so it is one happy bunny.

Thus, you are walking and the stores to purchase a bit of food and stressing about needing to purchase the great makes and the less expensive cuts of meat and worrying about your debt. You look from the region of your eye, and you are not sure what made you look, though you visit a bus coming straight at you.

Guess What Goes on Today?

Your unconscious mind moves into survival mode. You are in danger of dying, and you do not need to request assistance from your subconscious.

Within a millisecond, it beats your heart more quickly to pump more blood close to your body. It raises your breathing rate to make sure your ligaments and muscles and tendons have sufficient oxygen to help you move from danger.

It fires your nerve synapses and brain function to check out all potential escape choices in milliseconds, and it causes you into motion to escape the bus by pumping significant levels of adrenalin in your bloodstream. It almost makes you forget about your money worries and forces you to focus on getting from the bus.

After the danger has passed and it is once again prevailed in its Primary Purpose of keeping you alive, it only keeps on keeping you in existence.

So Why Does not It Allow You to Take Out of Debt?

The answer is straightforward. Your unconscious mind understands a tangible concept as a "bus coming." It recognizes a tangible concept as "debt." It does not comprehend an intangible idea such as, "get me out of..."

Thus, constantly that you are concentrating on "getting away of debt," as much as your subconscious is worried, debt is what you would like. And therefore, debt is what you get.

Today let us use Positive Thinking to buy your unconscious mind concentrating on real remedies. Stop focusing on debt, getting out of, or some additional term that employs the term debt.

For months, weeks, or days, you have been thinking to yourself in one type or any other, "I am in debt, get me from debt, how can I get from debt, what am I going to do about debt?" Your unconscious mind has presented your primary focus.

Think Positive

What is the contrary of debt? Pick a yummy word, riches, total bank balance, monetary abundance; you might begin with, "enough money every month to meet my bills" if you are not yet confident adequate to believe the strength of positive thinking.

Before going to sleep, take 10 minutes to speak with your unconscious mind. Sit or lie somewhere silent, the bed is most likely best, but if your partner won't interrupt or disrupt you.

Close your eyes and make a selection of extremely deep breaths. Breathe in through your nose for a count of five and breathe out through your mouth for a count of eight to ten. Repeat this ten times and ensure you empty your mind of any bad thought.

The first couple of times you practice this technique, you might be enticed to snigger or giggle to yourself. You might feel a bit of light-headed. That is completely fine because at the very least you have stopped worrying about your money troubles for some time.

Today, out loud, talk to your unconscious mind. Tell your unconscious mind that your lack of money is causing you stress. I ensure that your unconscious mind will sit straight up and listen to that particular statement.

You'll most likely see a marked slowdown inside your heart rate immediately. That is an indication that your unconscious mind is centered on that statement. Your unconscious mind understands "stress," alright!

Today, once again, out loud, inform your unconscious mind you require its help in locating a way to... [have your phrase prepared and don't make use of the term debt!]....e.g. carry you monetary abundance.

Specify an amount of money and specify a time and date you want this money. Highlight the term need. Tell your unconscious mind you insist that a fix is made known for you if you wake the next day.

Try keeping it true. Should you will need 500 dollars by 10 a.m. early in the day to pay your rent, you are not searching for help from your unconscious mind, you are searching for a miracle. You need to have maybe begun this exercise a few weeks ago if your financial need is that urgent.

You were not to understand this particular method, but all the same, you will have to sort that out on your own in the early morning. Nevertheless, making use of this technique to be able to get the following months' rent should do the job great.

If you wake up the next day, you will be pleasantly surprised to discover some good thoughts, and the prospective solution has been sent to you. All that is required then is the essential action. The answer might take you out of your comfort zone.

It might not be a palatable fix. It may be hard work, and it might be a time-consuming solution, though the answer would have been sent to you since your unconscious mind will have used every one immense power to locate the perfect solution.

It has not accomplished it for your benefit. It is done it since you informed it the scenario was causing you anxiety, and that is not congruent with its Primary Purpose.

The method will work for any circumstance that is causing you grief. In a later posting, I am going to talk a bit about how even your most harmful practices are assisted and abetted by the unconscious mind in its mistaken belief that those practices are everything you need.

CHAPTER 11

Whole Brain Thinking for Businesspeople

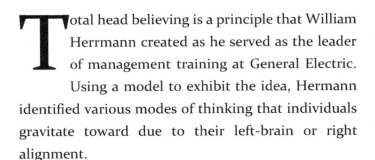

Total head believing is a principle that William Herrmann created as he served as the leader of management training at General Electric. Using a model to exhibit the idea, Hermann identified various modes of thinking that individuals gravitate toward due to their left-brain or right alignment.

Nowadays, Herrmann's Brain Dominance Model is among the most often used leadership development sources for integrated thinking. The modes of thinking the unit identifies are:

Analytical Thinking - A quantitative design of believing that concentrates on information gathering, using facts to judge, and rational reasoning.

Sequential Thinking - A thinking that is more structural, gravitating towards organization, directions, and details.

Interpersonal Thinking - A feeling based design of believing that favors: using the senses, expressing ideas, and looking for individual significance.

Innovative Thinking - A type of thinking that is imaginative and prefers: checking out the real picture, difficult assumptions, and thinking metaphorically.

Sequential thinking and analytical thinking are timeless modes of left-brained individuals, while right-brained people display interpersonal thinking and imaginative thinking.

Following subjects complete a questionnaire that reveals their style of thinking, they could concentrate on maximizing their cerebral strengths and becoming more experienced in styles of believing that aren't dominant parts of their mental profile.

In a company environment, people who apply the whole mind thinking (i.e., incorporated believed modes) have a good effect on specific and group productivity, thus the benefits of like the Brain Dominance Model with a company's leadership development resources.

The Positives for Businesses

For companies, the objectives of integrating believed modes are increasing efficiency by eliminating the conflicts that come from opposed believed modes and cultivating personnel that is capable of a few modes of thinking. When they rightly integrate thought modes, workers produce the following benefits for their employers.

Easier Job Matching - Matching job applicants with employment is a struggle that each business faces. When a candidate's thinking is mode dominating, it is usually difficult to match him or her with a task in that he or she accomplishes a lot of efficiencies. Growing his or her thought modes of her will make him or her a candidate for more positions.

Improved Strategic Planning - Group people that realize each other's predominant believed modes might find it a lot easier to create strategic plans. Ideas can be devised that mirror the short-term and long-term preparation types of various notion modes.

Improved Morale - Employees and company leaders that communicate well enhance the morale at the office. Right now, there are fewer disagreements, and consensuses are a lot easier to reach. Integrated thinking leads to better communication.

Whole-brain thinking is a principle that identifies the various modes in which individuals think analytically, interpersonally, sequentially, and imaginatively. By using info according to the Brain Dominance Model idea, organizations achieve the advantages mentioned above, among others.

To know more concerning the good effect that integrated believed modes have in-office use, call a provider of leadership development resources.

Consider the whole brain. It may sound like an insult that an individual colleague may send to the then in a time of anxiety, though it describes one thing that not many workers practice integrated thinking based on William Herrmann's idea of whole mind thinking. Hermann's idea might raise some questions about precisely how it benefits employees and businesses; the answers listed below will be informative.

The idea is founded on the concept that different people have various concept types that effect: the way they communicate with one another, use problem solving, make plans, etc.

In a company establishing these various concepts, types can contrast one another or come together under the process of incorporated thought - a method that is often employed for management development.

There are many suggestions for integrating the thinking types mentioned above into whole mind thinking. Techniques that are used for management development include:

- ○ Opposite Functions - Thinking in different tactics.
- ○ Sensory Immersion - Engaging the senses in the ideation process
- ○ Changing Note Taking - Using blank paper and colored pencils for notes
- ○ Different positions - Working in various roles for a short time

These techniques, among others, help supervisors and staff initiates and keep integrated thinking.

What advantages does incorporated thinking have for companies?

Businesses benefit from incorporated thought in a few ways. For example, workers that apply integrated believed usually have fewer disagreements, that tend to make the strategic planning process smoother, and increases morale at the office.

Individuals who have mastered incorporated consideration are usually easier to match with employment positions, as they could adapt their style of thinking to the type that is perfect for the position.

Where Do Companies Receive Lessons in Integrated Thinking?

Some business organizations teach workers in incorporated thinking by employing a team facilitator, who is taught in the subject. The teaching isn't carried out in one exercise session. However, the suggestions of the facilitator are taken far from the conference and applied in shorter sized education times inside the business.

Total head believing is a principle THAT William Herrmann produced as he served as General Electric's leader of management training. Nowadays, the idea was expanded into different knowledge programs that help interaction for the workplace, help with strategic planning, boost morale in-office use, and eventually build companies more productive.

CHAPTER 12

Logical Thinking - Can It Be Bad or Good?

Jean Piaget, one of the many founders of psychology, determined the threshold of rational thinking in the final phases of cognitive development.

At the concrete functional stage, Piaget observed logical thinking becomes evident in a kid's potential to use appropriate reason. The reason is characterized by ideas, reasoning, judgment, facts, concepts, and conclusion, and it is among the principles of human intelligence.

I love describing reasoning as a precise analysis of difficulties from an objective point of view. Extremely rational thinkers are much smarter and have remarkable decision making and problem-solving abilities. It is famous if a person practices rational thinking, he or she may become smarter.

At the same time, rational thinking has its limitations depending on the structural requirements, the exclusion of emotional intelligence; and the generalization required.

Structural Requirements

Rational thinking is related to atheism; In my opinion, this is an outcome of the narrow thinking required in reason. I mention this as rational thinking incorporates ideas, facts, concepts, and conclusions.

The reason involved in ideas, facts, concepts, and conclusions is created in a precise analytical fashion. Put, rational thinking is narrow in the feeling that reason demands building.

For instance, when solving a math problem, to get the appropriate answer, you need to do computations in a precise fashion, working with organized formulas. There is no deviating from the organized steps and formulas to get the appropriate answer.

In comparison, several logical thinkers will only have confidence in intangible reality; they have to consider it to think it. It is impossible, if not hard, for some rational thinkers to deviate from physical reality or to have confidence in the unseen.

Mental Intelligence

Logic is referred to as abstract thinking or a more significant form of thought; it is the ability to get emotionally independent by excluding emotional intelligence or emotions.

Making decisions and judgments with no mental attachments is an essential tool, particularly for individuals who are mentally challenged or suffer from anxiety and depression.

Feelings can cloud our thinking leading to bad judgment and decision making. Remember, emotional intelligence is crucial in developing relationships that are healthy. Therefore, logic alone does have its limits.

Generalization

Rational thinking leads to the generalization that is usually used in scientific techniques of reasoning. An overall idea, proposition, principle, law, statement, or concept is used broadly to evaluate a hypothesis, to assure a generalized truth. Generalization is akin to stereotyping that we know might have a destructive influence on society as a whole.

Without logic, it will be hard to perform simple tasks like cooking or planning our day. Rational thinking is crucial for reasoning, problem-solving, and decision making processes. Reason allows us to become mental independent, so our emotion doesn't wreak havoc in our lives.

Just like the rest in life (excluding energy), there are limits; rational thinking is restricted to its basic needs that exclude emotional intelligence. The generalization associated with reason doesn't account for the many little choices that, in my opinion, is a kind of narrow thinking.

To respond to the question, "logical thinking, can it be great or bad?" It is both bad and good; there are an area and time for everything; it is about harmony.

CHAPTER 13

Prosperity Thinking and How Can I Believe that Way?

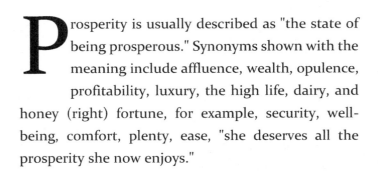

Prosperity is usually described as "the state of being prosperous." Synonyms shown with the meaning include affluence, wealth, opulence, profitability, luxury, the high life, dairy, and honey (right) fortune, for example, security, well-being, comfort, plenty, ease, "she deserves all the prosperity she now enjoys."

Even though the definitions and several in social consumption "prosperity" as a guide to economic gains and riches. There is an associated school of thought that broadens the prosperity framework of prosperity financially but to add a method of being called "prosperity mindset." This is speaking about the ability to open your whole life by way of a lens of prosperity in your thinking.

This is significant because studies have proven an excellent bulk of humans believed is negative, and that is the complete opposite of prosperity thinking.

There is a multitude of research demonstrating negative thinking is more typical to the man being, which could imply prosperity/positive thinking, and the concept isn't reasonable to the human being.

- 80 % of human thoughts each day are negative

- Our attitudes tend to be more severely affected by bad news than good news - in the English dictionary, 62 % are damaging mental words vs. 32 % sure words (

- 75-98 % of physical and mental illnesses are available from our thought life!

From my years of review, learning, and working in personal development and growth, psychology, coaching, and counseling, some ideas go on the top that will help you shift your thinking to a more prosperous brain.

The worth of this is not suitable for your mood and internal well-being but influences you physically and ripples into the remainder of your life (attraction and actions).

Some may find the subject of good psychology to feel 'rosy thinking," or improbable; nonetheless, when individuals find themselves around negativity, depressed, trapped, and continuously fighting "funks," these basic methods can alter their life.

You will find publications that dig deeper into the subject, but for the benefit of introduction, below are three components I have found to be crucial to growing and developing your prosperous mind.

1. Growth or Fixed Thinking. To get a prosperous brain - you wish to have FIXED THINKING vs. Growth Thinking. This idea is more normally presented in the academic and education community,

Nonetheless, it is a basis of learning and a primary mode of thinking, learning, and growing that is true for your whole life.

2. Abundance vs. Scarcity.

To use a Prosperity Mindset, examine what is Possible vs. what is NOT POSSIBLE. Abundance indicates that it is adequate, and there is a lot; it trusts that no matter what is has perfection to it. It creates confidence and contentment of acceptance to see the worth and benefit of what is. Scarcity concentrates on what we don't have and that it is not sufficient.

It produces a fear of the absence and creates a panic to take or get since there won't be adequate, or I may not have adequate. Due to our negative normal human wiring, it is normal to watch the world and life from a sacristy viewpoint.

For instance, two kids are sharing and think, if I do not get the toy I need now, I may not get it. As an adult, if you do not get a task you use for scarcity worries, I will not get a task or did badly.

The distinction is plenty of mindsets that have overlaps or similarities with the development mindset views it differently. Abundance knows I am going to have time together with the toy sometime. Abundance knows if I continue attempting, I am going to get the best job at the right time. In my experience, abundance vs. scarcity is all about trust vs. fear.

3. Unattachment vs. connection.

Finally, unattachment is the ability to let a thing go, and if it is intended to be, it will come back. Attachment is one method of seeing, doing, and thinking something. The attachment has been attached to my way. I have a preconceived idea of how it is going and appear, and if it doesn't occur in that way, I view it as a failure.

Unattachment sets goals, and they have visions but is ready to accept how things could evolve or unfold. THAT doesn't mean getting off course or ten instructions; it means being versatile to opportunities and possibilities as they present themselves and being open adequate to identify them while they may not be everything you expected. For instance, you really would like a task at Apple, but don't buy it.

You are provided the chance to volunteer at the high school and assistance with the tech club that could be a chance to take action associated with your goal and make contacts that could allow you to reach your main goal d the road. Usually, better opportunities than we can imagine present themselves. This is about your attitude.

A great method to check your thinking is writing your goals than five ideas about your goals. Place them through the air filter, and ensure they are growth-minded, have a prosperity viewpoint, and surrender attachments.

If the thoughts tend to be more fixed, scarcity, and then attached, create a T chart and create a good perspective on the opposite side. You could start training your thinking and shift the strategy you think, feel, and react to the world. The advantages won't bring more energy and joy to your life, but the

134 | William Bell

impact you have on others will be significant and noticeable too.

CHAPTER 14

Strategic Thinking

These are the five components that constitute strategic thinking and are:

- Intention focused
- A systems perspective
- Thinking in Time
- Smart Opportunism
- Hypothesis-driven

Among the frustrations I have had with the majority of the strategic planning definitions is the fact that seldom is the idea "strategic thinking" or "strategic" well defined.

In most definitions, strategic planning is described as a method that uses "strategic "strategies." or thinking," I suppose the definers think people inherently understand approach when they view it.

A tautology is a description that uses similar or the same conditions to describe what it implies, such as calling strategic planning a preparation process that creates strategies.

So what are these five important components of strategic thinking that she selected?

1. Intent Focused

Strategic intent offers the emphasis that allows people inside a company to leverage and marshal their energy, to completely focus attention, to withstand distraction, and to focus for so long as it takes to attain a goal."

This particular idea suggests both creating an overarching objective or guidance (you may call that your vision) and making that goal a calculated emphasis or, in this fantastic characterization, for intent. I discovered online "the action of switching the mind toward" an object or an outcome.

In the approach to our sector, this intent will be the change that we wish to consider in the world. A difference that we are enthusiastic about that channels our every activity for the future.

2. A Devices Perspective

Consider the environment.

An exercise I do with the graduate students you can try out for your organization is describing all the different methods that you are available. Their solutions begin with the classroom and go beyond the advanced schooling system, to legitimate, all-natural, home life, or body systems, to worldwide economic and monetary systems -- and so they run in most of them.

So does your organization. Thus, getting great at strategic thinking, you have to attempt to recognize the manner your world works and how that impacts you.

Because you cannot understand everything, you will need to get your best shot at collecting the correct info and prioritizing the parts of methods that are more than likely to influence the strategy you are working right now and into the world.

It does help though being curious about almost anything.

While you may be an authority in interpreting the specific "business ecosystem' that you operate, how well will you fully understand what is going on politically or culturally that may affect your future?

Read through a lot. Check out new things. Talk to individuals outside your organization and outside your discipline, and the individuals who know your system the best.

3. Thinking in Time

"Having noticed the potential future that we would like to create, what should we continue from our past, drop out of that past and make in the current to become there?"

When you think strategically, you are constantly linking the past to the current to the future. You learn from yesteryear and start using that learning how to make predictions. You glance at the present to look at the gap between the place you are where and now you wish to give up.

While your focus is constantly on the long term, you can act in the existing.

4. Intelligent Opportunism

Recall the outdated exercise the SWOT analysis (Strengths, Opportunities, Weaknesses, Threats.)

Effectively, SWOT thinking never ends for strategic thinkers. Strategic thinkers are in a position to notice and respond to wonderful new possibilities while they occur. They know that the world is dynamic, and they are ready to accept a change to reach the vision.

Intelligent opportunism likewise implies you dig deep into your organization to hear from many perspectives. Ideas and knowledge are important wherever they exist -- though you will have to look and listen to gain from them.

5. Hypothesis-driven

As strategic thinkers, we produce hypotheses, those that start "What if...?" or "If... then?" -- concerns that allow us to picture many scenarios, analyze them as best we can depend on the understanding we have amassed then evaluate the best hypotheses (experiment). As we act, we considered through our experience to produce a new hypothesis for future action.

CHAPTER 15

Energetic Thinking

W̱e are now living in an era of over-blown activity; almost everywhere you use, there is an increased focus on action-based lifestyle. Nevertheless, activity isn't necessarily productive; some people take part in a never-ending activity with nothing to show because of it, this is because they believe actively rather than productively.

Energetic thinking causes one to become engaged in most times and things without bringing out tangible outcomes; you can call it examination paralysis. The society and academic institutions encourage this particular type of thinking that is precisely why individuals are encouraged to go to college and blend into the culture by getting a 9 to 6 labor.

Regrettably, energetic thinking subtly stunts your growth and limits your ability to different birth things. Consequently, it becomes vital that you take proactive thinking a notch higher by doing hands-on thinking.

Hands-on believing will be the ability to originate a set of views and systematically convert them into modern physical outcomes. It can be considered being effective in your thinking, that is thinking of ways to invent, innovate, and produce new ways and products of doing things. Hands-on thinking doesn't imagine but translates each thought into action.

But there are strategic tricks that will transcend your thinking from that of regular energetic thinking on the one of proactivity, therefore, yielding limitless types of innovation, productivity, and inventions. There are lots of them, although five below are foundational ones and the core.

Try to Get Out of the CROWD:

The world is crowded, there is much noise everywhere, out of social networking to the workplace and family life, and there is an increasing presence of damaging delightful distractions.

These distractions lessen the quality of time individuals offer to believe, a lot of belief because of their eyes glued to their phones, their ears plugged

142 | William Bell

with audio from the earpiece and their thoughts on a million and one things at the identical time.

These make it extremely tricky to think through a concept and clear the fogs close to it. It has been established that thinking in a peaceful environment produces a better and clearer insight into anything.

A study has proven that ultra-creative and productive individuals have laser concentration skills, and they accomplish that by eliminating every type of distraction about them.

They intentionally move far from the group and take some time to mentally examine thoughts and appear to be deeply into them after that they turn out to place them into action. You as well could do this.

Write YOUR Thoughts Down:

To be prosperous in your thinking, you need to pen down your thoughts. There is this incredible vibe that comes from documenting what you are wondering. Most excellent inventions and innovation came as an outcome of deliberate documentation of thoughts and insights about concepts and ideas.

Typically incredible insights flash through our minds if we don't record them; the odds are high that they'll be forgotten. Even if you are not sure if they will work, or if they are practical, make sure you create them down after some time goes through them once again, you'll be so astonished the way a new dimension of it comes up.

Documenting focuses and imprints them in our subconscious mind without our understanding, the brain is structuring, developing, and working them into practical ideas. My advice has a note pad as often as you can.

Talk About IT:

One hands-on strategy to think well and better is talking about your ideas. I understand this seems challenging, though it is really good to go over your ideas and concepts with somebody you believe in and hold in high esteem.

A guide is regarded as an excellent individual to accomplish this with since he will help you iron through a few rough edges and mention mistakes in the idea.

Nevertheless, discussing your ideas with individuals can be quite sticky, since most will misunderstand you, and you'll most likely look too advanced and arrogant. Therefore there is a twist for this, and it is advisable so that you can subtly inject your ideas in interactions without allowing others to know.

This can allow you to know their unknown compromised reactions to the idea and determine if they had believed in such direction earlier. Another thing is to discuss those ideas you have gone seventy % into, not formless ones.

Issue YOURSELF:

A strategic strategy to clean up the misunderstandings surrounding anything is asking yourself questions. Introspection is the primary key to self-discovery and the catalyst for productivity and change. Thus, think about questions relating to your thoughts; this will assist you in cleaning the assumptions you are more likely to harbor in your subconscious.

If you challenge yourself, you are placing yourself on the edge of discovery, since one right answered rightly is a milestone to getting a tangible consequence. Question your assumptions towards the concept, question what am I ignoring that I'm meant knowing, use, or investigation on, with which an innovative ray of options would arise.

BE Ready To Accept Possibilities:

Living includes serendipity; one quest can be a life-altering voyage; thus, be ready to accept twists, turns, down-hills, and up-hills the idea is with.

One action can wreck everything you worked quite difficult for; an additional could make you come to be an overnight wonder to the whole world. In the root cause of searching for something else, most excellent innovators and inventors stumbled on one more thing, which brought about their eureka moments.

Who inspires my friend Archimedes the solution he sought after would be found out inside a bathroom, emanating from a bucket? No one knew, so also, you don't understand, neither do I understand what that concept you have right this moment will birth into truth. Come with an open mind for options.

The distinction between energetic thinking and practical thinking is ACTION. Step through and indulge your thoughts in real-life events. In that way, you learn the things that work and what does not.

Many people have impressive concepts with them, though they are doing nothing about them and so the ideas lie useless and dormant. The sole means to consider if what you are thinking could be done is by acting it out there.

William Shakespeare earlier wrote,' ACTION Is ELOQUENCE' so, think through a concept and begin taking deliberate, calculated actions. The core secret is to believe and act together, don't wait around to determine all rather begin from the known, and surely you will get towards the unfamiliar.

CHAPTER 16

Higher-Order Thinking

In the last several centuries, we have discovered medical breakthroughs. We have engineered devices THAT could do things we cannot do. We have created laws to advance our society. We have designed computers to make our lives more effective. We have created a lot of technological advances, have we not?

Basically, no, we did not make them at all. Considerable contributions to technical change have been created by under one % of the public. The rest of us stick to the lead of people who produce the change.

So what is the big difference between individuals who stick to the switch (followers) people who apply them (middle males) and people who produce them (leaders and experts)?

The most popular response to this is the difference is dependent upon what an individual understands. Expertise with no wisdom, however, is

148 | William Bell

unhelpful. It is how an individual applies the knowledge that determines their success.

The application of such knowledge boils d to a simple, however often overlooked idea called thinking. It is not what we think about also, but how we consider it.

Explorative Learning - Asking the right questions.

Here is something to think about: like people stay away from exercise since it exhausts the whole body, the same holds for how thinking exhausts the brain. We like models to work for us only as we choose a person to explain a thing to stay away from the hassle of finding it out.

But as exercising makes the whole body stronger, a good mind should also have the best sort of regular' thinking' workouts. A personal Trainer might direct our progress by setting the process but would do nothing if they raise the weights for us. Furthermore, an excellent instructor wouldn't count on sound understanding to be accomplished by an explanation by itself.

If the learner has explored the idea at deeper and deeper progressively levels, the explanation THAT follows will create a more good significance than what it had without' thinking it through' initially.

It means that the most effective explanations are those that join the majority of rightly with the questions they preceded., it means that the most effective teachers are people who recognize how you can facilitate learning by asking the right questions.

What Are the Right Questions?

Great question. The solution is Higher Order Thinking thoughts, although to be able to realize the solution, we should initially ask additional questions to explore this particular idea deeper.

What Kinds of Questions Can Be Found?

The level (or thoroughness) of our comprehension is driven by the level our thought processes undergo while studying it.

At the shallow end, we discover the considerably more simplistic thinking procedures, including recollection, comprehension, and some form of program. Having the ability to explore questions created at these amounts are required to get a fundamental understanding when studying new ideas.

Building simple power to produce exceptional achievement, however, demands to delve steadily more deeply into exploration by getting the' Higher Order Thinking' procedures, for example, analysis, creativity, and evaluation (sometimes described as' critical thinking').

Blooms' Taxonomy - A Model for Higher Order Thinking Skills (HOTS) The cognitive URL of Blooms' Taxonomy may be the most widely known unit used in Educational Psychology for categorizing the level and levels of consideration active in the learning operation. As the level of understanding increases, therefore, does the capabilities the learner has the ability to demonstrate.

Knowledge: Remembering facts, dates, locations, names, terms, basic concepts, and sequences.

Comprehension: Demonstrating an understanding of the info recalled by looking at and planning it into something significant.

Application: Using that understanding coupled with methods to resolve an issue or finish a job.

Analysis: Breaking info down into elements for examination to establish connections and causes.

Evaluation: Using the result of analyses making conclusions about something is worth base choices on.

Creation: Connecting the significance of evaluations to synthesize new ideas or new concepts THAT need constant evaluation and analysis (thus continuing the cycle).

Mediocrity to Excellence - From the Classroom on Real-life Memory, comprehension, and software are essential thinking abilities, all of us need understanding and finish basic tasks, pass assessments, and hold down a standard job.

In a workplace setting particularly, Critical or' Higher Order' Thinking skills (analysis, analysis, and creation) are most highly used in roles offered to individuals charged with the duty of making very important choices.

Managers, for instance, might have to assess prospective applicants and then assess who to employ and fire. Right after examining each element involved and analyzing the probable effect on future changes, it is the duty of those largest in command (leaders) to make use of inventive operations for revolutionary uses.

Examples could include establishing new policies, setting up new job descriptions, creating new instruction resources, developing new marketing methods, and or inventing new products. Due to how Higher Order Thinking Skills sort mediocrity from excellence in the qualified world, Assessors work with identical versions to establish benchmarks for being successful at school also.

The greater crucial assessment responsibilities (especially from HSC level) are sometimes created not only to assess the breadth of any student's expertise, though the level of their understanding. In reality, assessment concerns that take the heaviest weighted marks are those based around analysis, creation, and evaluation.

Higher Order Thinking Skills Activities in the House

Because we quite often wish to make sure our kids reach the' right conclusion,' it is appealing to explain anything instead of letting them enjoy their thoughts about the subject.

The easiest ways where parents can help in creating a child's Higher Order Thinking abilities is often as easy as encouraging our children to think about' why," how' and' therefore what this means is that...'

Because their comprehension is made around a constructivist framework, the best teachers will steadily deepen your kid's comprehension through the use of Higher Order Thinking thoughts to examine the learning processes one level at the same time.

This particular procedure steadily constructs understanding to understanding, and understanding into the experience. In the temporary, your child's assessment marks will soar. In the very long term, so also will their future success.

Even though culture and language affect how your kid's higher-order thinking skills are produced, the greater order thinking activities must be adapted based on the learning environment.

CHAPTER 17

Thinking Outside
of the Tightest Box

As info changes faster, there is more conversation about thinking outside of the box. We usually mean by this to consider standard things in new ways. Like for example, is marriage as sacred as we have consistently been taught it is or would like to perform more effectively if it had been identified in an adaptable fashion?

Or is driving automobiles on hydrogen or vegetable oil as practical alternatives to traditional oil treatments as a few claim them to be-to note a few of extremely debatable issues?

We are acquiring more accustomed to thinking about things in provocative and unexpected methods' capacity to understand new choices.

But strangely enough, barely anyone is spending a lot focus on thinking beyond the greatest, tightest package of them all ourselves. Oh, we get it done in

Mental Models | 155

like for the benefit of all we are concerned about, unwillingly, and at minimum to the degree that they demand us to adjust. And quite often, it creates a tremendous alteration in stretching the envelope of our life.

Though we do not get it done, especially on be that extends our half-elves, not with the same energy that we get it done for all the other subject matter in our imaginative mind.

Surely it appears to be disloyal to others to step far outside the box of who we are unless they have requested for it. Individuals count upon us to remain the same, to stay recognizable. When we alter excessively, they feel abandoned.

The process obstacle to better stepping outside of the box elf is we view it to be nearly completely an exercise of believing.

The rise of objectivity on the kingly position of dominance in our common philosophical perspective and that underlies the belief in "facts," has produced from our conviction that science is practically completely about reasoning and measuring. We feel the brain can record the significance of anything; hence, to modify something, one should believe differently.

Psychology has proved this to become an utterly wrong premise. But because the systematic research of selfness is still a stepchild to medication, meaning good for understanding pathology, consequently, it is essentially ignored in a philosophical area.

And yet, as every great psychotherapist understands, in the human psyche info is coded mentally, not intellectually.

To produce a paradigmatic change in our understanding about something demands a mental movement that occurs intuitively and spontaneously, not by reason or its measurements,although reason might have brought us, at different times, around the potential for a perspective shift though it cannot take us all the way.

Creative thinking can occur mathematically to a complicated mathematician. Although in that case, it too derives not only from thinking mathematically but, and principally from an intuitive method that includes a mental shift of perspective-one that instructs the brain with a new concept or equation. Simply put, the brain is the final to consider anything.

Hence it does not control the procedure of learning. Indeed it is the fortunate receiver of that process. Its "control" powers, of that we are so enamored as technologists, adopt from that instruction.

Put, the brain, when given a new idea, is quite clever at finding unlimited uses of that new info. The brain is thus not the originator of info as we are fond of believing. It is the engineer of discovered consent capable of using it endlessly.

If a person would like to considerably expand the capacity for paradigmatic shifting in their understanding of daily life, one should, above any other topics, examine the self. The biggest problem in doing this is it is not feasible to do it alone, at least not even, until we hugely create the whole arena of self-understanding. For the current day, we want a partner. Ideally, one rightly trained in assisting somebody to consider themselves.

Sadly the sole individuals with this particular ability are experts that promote themselves as healers of mental illness. Thus we have to admit we are insane before they assist us. Precisely what an unfortunate state of affairs if the most crucial learning of all should be defined in this humiliating manner.

We are therefore left to dwell in the family member's ignorance of our current models of self-understanding. The most popular practice is usually to ignore the self as a topic of study.

Many people invest their whole lives in social experience, performing the points they can do with many other individuals, typically perceiving aloneness as being a curse that should be treated as urgently as you can.

Hence they are cursed by being completely caught to the package of themselves that others have programmed at the start of their life, ever getting the opportunity to self-determine how who and what they are in many the most potent and crucial methods.

A man is an ecosystem that is recognized and unknown components. Fundamentally we still do not have confidence in the unconscious, except philosophically, that means in principle, however, not in reality.

As proof, we do not walk around realizing there are important, if not big, parts elves we do not comprehend well, areas that remain hidden behind different screens of secrecy, fear, and loyalty to search too heavily.

Nobody walks by life unscathed without the marks of some unacknowledged adversity or nightmare that was character developing. The popular and huge plethora of horror films verifies this assertion; they companion and present our hidden terrors, with that we are secretly obsessed; still, individually understand little about.

We are currently learning how to be any human means. We pretend we know earlier. But so long as we hide from substantial parts elves, we will remain unaware of the reality, and caught in the box were another person place us.

CHAPTER 18

Mental Models for Learning Organizations

———————⟨⟩⟨⟩———————

"My supervisor never listens to whatever I have to say. He will request my opinion and then do what he intended to. Why do I need to bother?"

"Most of my employees do not care much about their work. The one thing that appears to encourage them would be the conclusion of the week. Guess I will have to undertake it myself."

Seem familiar? Those are two various views of an identical situation. They are mental versions in motion, and they bolster a terrible pattern of behavior that is ultimately destructive to a company in many ways.

What are the mental models?

Mental Models | 161

These models are deeply ingrained generalizations or assumptions influence how we understand the world and take action. Other words we use for mental models are mindset, assumptions, beliefs, and perspectives, to name a few.

Mental models are usually the most significant barriers to applying new concepts in organizations, though they are part of learning where organizations can make a significant influence.

Regrettably, assumptions, the term usually used to relate to mental models, have a bad connotation to the majority of us. We have all noticed the old saying, "You know what occurs when you believe? It will make a ____ from you and me."

Effectively, you can fill up in the blank. Assumptions, nevertheless, are the sole way we can make sense of our complex world. It is not feasible to get information that is complete about every scenario we face; therefore, by their nature, assumptions, or mental models are unfinished and subsequently flawed. For the most part, nonetheless, our mental models serve us very well.

You will find occasions where our mental models tend to lead us astray. A perfect example of how imperfect mental models will be is produced by the early parable of the blind men and the elephant, in which many blind men feel various areas of an elephant and describing it.

The information on them is incorrect, but when put together in one, provide a better, albeit still flawed explanation of what an elephant is like. Mental models are puzzle pieces that we have to fit together into a bigger whole.

As various mental models are recognized, another portion falls into spot, and we come across a better picture, but in this particular work, we don't possess the roof of the puzzle package to direct us. We need to grope along just like the blind men.

Mental models impact what we come across in situations and make reinforcing patterns of behavior. In the illustration provided at the start of the chapter, the employee views a domineering and managing manager, even though the supervisor sees personnel who wish to invest the bare minimum.

As an outcome, the workers start to be disengaged, and the supervisor tries to micromanage more - not an extremely effective situation in any business.

Mental Models | 163

The greater the manager tries to manage the situation, the greater the disengaged the workers become, resulting in an adversely reinforcing cycle. The noticeable portion of the cycle, the actions, reinforces the invisible part, mental models, or the beliefs.

What skills do people have to develop?

How does one break from this particular kind of downward spiral?

The first action is recognizing the gap between what we feel to be genuine and what is true, or setting it more, the gap between current reality and mental models. You will find two primary parts of abilities where people can practice working for mental models:

Abilities of reflection and

Skills of inquiry.

Abilities of reflection involve slowing our thinking to ensure we start to be more conscious of how we develop our mental models and how they affect our behavior. We can accomplish this in a few ways.

One of the ways is becoming more conscious of recognizing when we create what is known as "leaps of abstraction," which is making generalizations according to our observations without any information to support it.

In the manager-employee instance, the worker observes the supervisor requesting a viewpoint, however, not acting upon it. The employee then jumps towards the realization that the manger is not interested in subordinates' suggestions.

In turn, the supervisor observes disengagement and concludes it should be as the workers do not care about their work. A good way to stay away from this pitfall is asking the questions:

"What is the information on that my beliefs or generalizations are based?"

"Have I noticed any disconfirming proof of my beliefs?"

"Am I prepared to consider the chance that my beliefs might be inaccurate?"

An additional means for building abilities of reflection is known as exposing the "left-hand column." The "left-hand column" symbolizes thoughts we quite often have during interact

By really writing these thoughts down immediately after the simple fact, we are making our mental models visible. For instance, the manager that

Mental Models | 165

views his employees as demotivated could announce a meeting of the department to discuss a new strategic direction for his team.

Right after presenting the concept, he asks for a response, and it is greeted with stony silence. His instant thought might be, "Man! What is it likely to shoot lighting a fire under these people?"

If a worker does respond with tepid assistance, he may also believe, "Oh geez! Right here, we choose the lip service once again! Cannot they believe for themselves?"

Each one of these reactions reinforces the manager's brain design, but writing them down helps it be easy for him to distance himself enough from the perception to start to realize it for what it is, a generalization.

The last method for building abilities of manifestation recognizes the gap between what we say we feel, our espoused concept, and what we do, our theory in use. Put an additional way; we must begin comparing our words to our behaviors or actions.

Using the manager-employee example again, the supervisor may think that participative decision-making produces a productive team, though his behavior isn't sending that message to his employees. Until he knows that gap, no change or learning can occur.

Abilities of inquiry shape how we operate in face-to-face interactions. After we have begun practicing our skills of reflection, we can then start to surface and discuss our mental models with other people. In doing this, we must recall that our mental models are pieces on the puzzle.

As a Skilled Facilitator, Roger Schwarz has created a method known as mutual learning design that may assist people to sharpen their interpersonal skills.

It is based on the assumption that everybody sees things differently, and it is the differences that create opportunities for creativity and learning. It is depending on the perception that everybody is acting with integrity. One may perform the mutual learning model by:

To test your assumptions by articulating them and requesting verifying or disconfirming evidence;

Sharing all pertinent information: withholding information is only going to result in a less complete picture;

Being transparent by putting the thinking on the table rather compared to your finished thought;

Concentrating on interests, that is, not positions, discussing and coming to an agreement to outcomes before arriving at solutions;

Talking about those ideas in the "left-hand column" that are typically operating your actions; Balancing advocacy with an inquiry, that is, asking about other factors of view almost as you clarify your abilities.

These abilities, in conjunction with the abilities of reflection, will unleash the ability to alter mental models and to start shifting the group toward sustainable change. To be able to change our behavior, we should alter the values in what those actions are based on.

How can organizations transform mental versions from barrier to use point?

Dealing with mental models is regarded as a hard place to begin building a learning organization but tends to yield the best level of change.

Shaping and developing mental models usually means replacing organizational behavior and both individual - a tall order at best. It is a method that requires perseverance and patience. The following conditions will help organizations lessen the barriers to examining and surfacing mental models:

Make a secure environment where workers feel comfy examining and surfacing their mental models; it should also be a world where choices are derived from what is ideal for the business, not on politics;

Help your workers develop their skills of inquiry; and reflection

Promote variety rather compared to conformity;

Agree to disagree; everybody doesn't have to go and the different mental models that exist; each one is an extra piece of info; Be at ease with uncertainty; we won't ever know the whole story.

This process requires organizations and individuals alike to change the way they consider the dynamics of work. When those obstacles are lowered, a company could start to observe mental models be leverage points for originality. Those bad reinforcing loops change into upward spirals of achievement.

CHAPTER 19

Mental Modeling
and Thought Chains

Deep breathing is the procedure of realizing one is an individual brain, intending to pursue your very Thought Chain to produce a functional Mental Model.

Our minds are active all the time. As we communicate with our environment, our minds are continuously producing thought chains. This can lead to a constant barrage of sound.

It is like getting a radio station, set on the same channel, playing in your head for eternity. Without the luxury of volume control or an on-off switch, you are lost. Yoga and meditation provide you with volume control and an on-off switch to use when you have to.

All our ideas and actions are made from these thought chains. We are literally what we feel. And so then it makes sense that we can consider understanding the way the mind works, finding out how our minds function, as something that is incredibly vital and to be taken seriously.

It bears repeating that this is what relaxation does. It is a method that relies upon a working model of how the minds work. Meditation is a method that lets us understand ourselves. Through meditation you can;

* Look at your thoughts,

* Look at the thoughts from the viewpoint of the observed, and the observer

* Discover ways to alter the strategy you believe, to be more productive,

* Recognize that the way you believe and communicate with the world, determine how sad or happy you are, and lastly,

* Realize the many physical and mental benefits that meditation and yoga provides.

Emotional activity creates thoughts that are linked together and other thoughts. Therefore, for example:

* You see someone who reminds you of a well-used friend called Bob,

* You think," I love Bob,"

* You think about what Bob is up to,

* You question how the existing gang is doing,

* You question whether Bob is on Facebook, * You go on to take a look at Facebook, to find your old friend Bob and all your other old friends from the gang.

And so, the first interaction with the atmosphere triggers a sure action. This is ordinarily the case. Firstly you respond to the person who reminds you of Bob. You respond to the exterior environmental stimulus.

You, the viewer, then go on to take notice of the stimulus and react. This particular activity triggers one more notion and reaction and observation, and an additional, and another.

You may also create thought chains THAT will ultimately result in an entirely different thought pattern or subject matter. For example:

* You begin seeing the person who reminds you of Bob,

* You observe you "like" Bob,

* Bob causes you to think good,

* You feel, "Bob was constantly in great shape, he usually exercised a lot,"

* You consider you individual bodily conditioning,

* You observe you are not especially excited about the form that you are in,

* This causes you to feel negative,

* You believe, "I must reach the fitness center and exercise harder."

* After this you observe, that causes you to feel great, though you do not have the time to reach the gym tonight since you have to work late,

* You subsequently observe you believe badly you will not be equipped to sort out tonight.

In the concept mentioned above chain, you went off subject, and you might have seen, you went from being great to being bad to feeling good to feeling terrible once again, everything within a couple of occasions. Yikes! Ridiculous right.

Still, this is what we do all the time. We always subject ourselves to this fruitless mental dance. Shifting from one chain of thoughts to the then, often without being informed of what is going on in us.

You have no clue how to end it, change it, and at the very least, not to get it to influence you in a bad manner. Occasionally you will act out without knowing what you are doing.

Through Meditation and Yoga, you will learn the right way to monitor your thought chains and recognize unproductive physical patterns in your thinking.

You will form a working model of how your mind functions, so you can quickly notice damaging concept chains and start creating new, good feelings to change them. You will move ahead with your life and manifest a vibrant and rewarding reality.

CHAPTER 20

Think Highly of Yourself

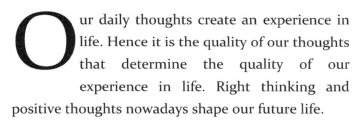

Our daily thoughts create an experience in life. Hence it is the quality of our thoughts that determine the quality of our experience in life. Right thinking and positive thoughts nowadays shape our future life.

Out of the 60,000 views that we feel one day, the vast majority of these opinions somehow center around the idea and ways we relate with the world. 90 % of these ideas are similar views we believed yesterday, and the majority of them are negative or non-productive. It shouldn't be surprising that for most of us, our experiences are much from satisfactory.

A study has shown that the majority of us use low opinion elves. We believe much fewer than is necessary or real. Other people's opinions about us usually form our opinion of ourselves.

Hence we start to be susceptible to the conflicting views others have of us. A lot of our energy is therefore expended living up to people's expectations of us. This particular, I have found, is an act of self-sabotage and must be remedied.

In most cultures, we are trained to be self-deprecating and modest. Placing ourselves down or underplaying our achievements is upheld as being a virtue. It is typical for also the successful and rich individuals to downplay their success to be regarded as modest and then to generate the value and approval of others.

Thoughts have the power and energy that they magnetize circumstances of energy that is similar in our life. What this means is that negative thoughts magnetize bad experiences to our life, while good thoughts magnetize good experiences.

Our level of accomplishment in life is straight proportionate to our self-image, which, in our opinion. If we believe we are not entitled to respect, success, and love, our belief will prove itself as being accurate in our experiences. When we choose to improve our opinions, we will develop the self-confidence to set higher goals and to attain them.

Whatever opinion you opt to have elf will be realized in life that is real. Every thought, belief or opinion, functions as a command on the subconscious mind, whose purpose is obeying and implement the command. The subconscious mind can't argue with any decision or thought you want to make; it cannot distinguish between what is genuine or imagined.

It is programmed to apply every thought. Consequently, if you opt to get a better opinion of yourself than is now accurate, the desire to be a better person is acted upon by the subconscious mind.

Consequently, all you have to accomplish is to think good thoughts about yourself continually and will come true in no time.

There is a force that shapes our lives. It determines what we think about impossible or possible, what you attempt or pull back from, the way you think, and interact. This particular force is the belief you have about who you are - your identity.

Whom we think or believe we are, affects every part of our lives. If you believe you dare not, then you won't ever try the initial step. If you suspect you can, your very will catapult you towards success.

Hence an alteration of your opinion will instantly alter your talents, behavior, and aspirations. It is through this belief that you interpret experiences of life.

Try defining yourself in an empowering method every day. In no time, you will surely be the way you describe yourself - I mean your ideal self. Avoid, no matter what defining yourself in ways that create limits to your achievement. Stay away from descriptions as "I am powerless at this," "I am gross." Remember, we hold the supreme power to define who we are.

After we can uphold these good picture elves with confidence, the world will accept the same meaning elves. Alternatively, if we carry on and hold low self-esteem, we can bet that the world will agree with us.

To be able to create a profound enhancement in the quality of our life, we should modify or grow our identity to one that moves us ahead towards a greater fulfillment of our life goals. Training thinking of yourself. Ensure your self-dialogue is good. Imagine yourself at your best always. Keep your head up high, walk taller. You are God's best creation.

CHAPTER 21

Mental Models: The Box Everyone Is Trying to Think Outside Of

How many times weekly does a company owner hear, "It is time to do a little exterior box thinking?" Mental versions would be the package everybody is attempting to get away. Mental models avoid thinking forward events. Private thought processes are built by perception, creativity, and understanding of the world.

An individual views a chocolate bar, and it is good. It is a candy bar, and could it be a cellular phone and have a candy bar case? The innovative mobile phone case was an opportune thinking forward event since it deconstructed a mental style.

The apparent use of mental versions is to an individual's perspective of her or himself about surroundings. Self-concept is built through perceived features, education, and social tasks. A lot of this self-concept results in subconscious assumptions.

Human assumptions spill over into the company. Nearly all businesses thrive on staying in front of the competition and comprehend that when complacency takes hold, competitive advantage will be lost. Company leader assumptions lead to coziness that produces a simplification of truth.

Often these assumptions render businesses caught in a similar site as innovation passes them by. Huge multi-channel corporations are particularly impacted by this particular phenomenon as personnel and management start to be a lot more and more disjointed from the bigger corporate mission.

Cross-matrix global businesses particularly have recognition for having become comfortable. "This is how it has constantly been done," is claimed again and again as organizations lose market share to unseen competition and innovation.

The story of the massive business that ignores advanced thinking functions, and it is consequently undercut by the small, but nimble, competition is told again and again in company colleges. The cure to shortsighted assumptions can be a dose of exterior package thinking. Outside box thinking can make the biggest companies nimble in their decision-making.

Humans are inherently flawed and need assistance anticipating upcoming company trends due to assumptive mental models. The picture of competition near a business that workers construct is a model. A definite choice for about any business is the answer to selecting exterior box thinking as a shelter against complacency, customer attrition, and brand equity loss.

Do not Hold back until You Require Corporate Emergency Triage

Occasionally the most out-of-the-box matter a business can do is look outside for assistance to develop a better sort of different. Not only outside the business but outside the market.

Almost as your company or business requires an innovation advisor, you have one that understands meaningfulness as foundation and stepping stone, not an afterthought.

Every company and industry has its culture that culture usually produces a type of "traditional target blindness." Precisely the same suggestions keep coming up since the same individuals are tasked with developing new ways to old issues. Nevertheless, ultimately, an enterprise innovates its way to the

Mental Models | 181

pinnacle of the market, or it stagnates its way into bankruptcy.

CHAPTER 22

Thinking of How We Think

In this particular chapter, I am going to attempt an evaluation of what Philosophers and even other thinkers, like myself, have developed regarding the methods where it is thought humans believe, and how those ideas have impacted the human ability to think rationally. In truth, the vast majority of adult people do little, if any, legitimate thinking in any way.

What passes for believing is made up of: daydreaming, worrying, planning, rehashing prior experiences of all types, etc., etc. The great majority of individuals aren't alert to what is happening in their minds at any time, not to mention to invest some time considering the way they think.

Socrates is quoted as having said, "An unexamined life isn't worth living." A brief search of the net will bring up many references to his, above quoted, declaration.

To claim that an individual may analyze one is life, implies thinking of it. As suggested, nevertheless, these days, it is a minority of people who could be stated to be imagining for brief times throughout the day, not to mention their lives.

To "think" implies processing info. Dictionary.com defines "thinking" as "rational; reasoning: People are thinking animals." Thinking, quite, having the ability to believe and cause, based on this definition, is what is designed to function as the determining element of the thing that makes humans, persons!

A person who is in a position to believe, and the reason is to be "rational." Conversely, a logical individual, is regarded as a "reasoning" individual. The word, "rational" is the root of, "rationale," the reasons given, or grounds for, behavior, beliefs, actions, etc., etc., in addition to, "rationalization"; one thing we humans are good at.

The debate of this kind is usually regarded as the province of Philosophy, and Philosophers do a lot of haggling regarding the topic of believing. It is time; nonetheless, this dialogue is used in place by the general public, particularly so as it is designed to be a defining element of what makes us human!

I, personally, am convinced that Philosophers have become poorly off track about this particular topic, having been affected by 18th Century thinkers.

Those Philosophers discovered that there were two primary types of thinking: Empirical Thinking, and Rational Thinking, each of which having now been changed by the dominance of Scientific Thinking.

Empirical thinking is regarded as imagining that often originates in, and is influenced by experience, and it is known as, "Empiricism," Empiricism, as suggested, is depending on the perception that what we individually experience, or have analyzed thoroughly, is a legitimate method of getting info about the earth around us.

Expertise based on Empiricism still lingers, so-called, in the, however, smooth Sciences. Smooth Sciences are becoming those that it might be hard, if not impossible, to create measurable criteria for conclusions.

"Rationalism," or rational thinking on the opposite hand, will be the Philosophical, "doctrine that reason by itself is a supply of understanding, and it is free from experience." Or as a broad definition, "The habit or principle of taking reason as the supreme expert of matters of conduct., belief, or opinion

Based on the Stanford Encyclopedia of Philosophy, "Rationalists maintain that you can find important ways where our concepts and understanding are achieved independently of feeling knowledge. Empiricists say that sense experience is the supreme cause of all our knowledge." and concepts

With all the arrival of "scientific" methods of gaining knowledge, in particular, Empiricism was attacked and debunked. Presently, in the cutting edge of these episodes would be the professional, "skeptics," who sneer at individuals that think that whatever they individually experience has validity.

Systematic thinking is the device that has changed Rationalism and Empiricism as a means of increasing understanding.

Scientific knowledge is acquired largely through experimentation with settings, (that which isn't affected by the part of what is being analyzed through experimentation). The systematic method entails the breaking down of everything into little factors, after that is checking out the elements.

Seldom is an effort made by the hard Sciences to learn the whole of anything at all, apart from, for instance, Astrophysicists. (Those sciences called, "soft" do make an effort in a holistic approach, like Ecologists, Anthropologists, Archaeologists, etc.)

Thus, utilizing the Scientific Method as an academic design, Scientific Thinking discourages a generalist and a holistic approach to gaining understanding.

Presently, what is deemed to be "Scientific Thinking" is building upon previous medical published writings as fact and authority? Effective young researchers continue to extrapolate from the identified information to add new awareness according to the existing.

Those newer Scientists that manage to have Doctorates in their field and who, subsequently, dare to challenge the Facts to have a problem getting their work published.

Within the last long, while a huge amount of this former, "fundamental" analysis has been discovered being flawed, if not a genuine fabrication.

This information hasn't been commonly dispensed, however. As to recent study, noted

Scientific Journals have must acknowledge that what is printed through the years has often been published by people who have received a vested interest in the result of their research.

Nevertheless, Scientific Thinking has become the overriding system that is taught in colleges and universities today. Hence, it is going to be the basis of any thinking presently being carried out by people who consider themselves educated.

The fundamental underlying structure of science is dependent on Reductionism, the perception that it is feasible to reach an understanding of the whole of whatever, by learning its parts.

Studying, "the whole of things" is left to Religion and philosophers; both parts deemed nonscientific and, by definition, without logical. Another main underpinning of science is the doctrine that that that they are learning is physical.

All people who haven't been indoctrinated into Scientific Thinking, by an overdose of training, will normally base their thinking on what they have discovered empirically.

Others, such as educated, but independent, Philosophers, like myself, have arrived at the realization that the whole procedure of Scientific Thinking is flawed, on account of these two standard underpinning premises.

The creation of the science, "Ecology," in the 1950s, for me, challenged the essential reductionist principal in the world recognized science. Dictionary.com defines, "Ecology" as: "the department of biology coping with the associations and interactions between organisms and their environment that includes different organisms."

The initial description remaining out humans included in the natural equation, a significant mistake, in my opinion. Subsequently, an additional class created, known as "Human Ecology, defined as the department of sociology, "concerned with the spacing and interdependence of institutions" and people.

There are additional ways, heading again in time, of Philosophers imagining about thinking that impact the number of men and women believe nonetheless today; among these may be the Philosophical writings of Aristotle.

Aristotle, among other philosophical ideas, introduced what is recognized now as the device of Logic. Based on the Stanford Encyclopedia of

Philosophy, "Aristotle's logic, particularly his theory of the syllogism, has had an unparalleled impact on the story of Western thought."

We have seen contemporary efforts to challenge the Aristotelian impact on thinking, the main one having been General Semantics, created by Alfred Korzybski, who published the book, Sanity. and Science (As I remember, Korzybski was a mathematician.) General Semantics was the self-called "A non-Aristotelian approach to finding out how folks think, and the many mistakes in the way individuals process inbound information."

Though the concept of having the ability to believe critically and clearly, can be traced back again at minimum as much as Aristotle, there continues to be a resurgence in the use of the word, "Critical Thinking" to the stage that an individual writer about the subject mentioned in the work that, "... in recent years' critical thinking' is now a thing of a' buzz word' in academic circles... "

CONCLUSION

A mental model is a chosen range of methods and beliefs to understand a sure context, underpinned by a less conscious paradigm or worldview.

Context is somewhat of a slippery term, but for our purposes, think of context as all the items that involve your teaching environment. Nowadays, the standard mental model of how teachers address the learning situation is under increasing scrutiny.

This is nothing new as there have usually been great debates more than educational methods. Nevertheless, we today have something new to think about - stylish scientific research on the way the brain learns. While not conclusive, this particular research supports the task of the conventional "teacher tell" strategy.

As a consequence, instructors and teachers in most educational venues are experimenting with various techniques of educating learners. Nevertheless, instructors are adopting new techniques without also analyzing their belief systems about what constitutes good training, particularly and the way the community in general functions.

If you feel a world with no structure and order results in chaos, how committed are you very likely to be too flipping over a whole workshop to team conversation strategies, role plays, and simulations?

You may think learners need some say in what it is they considered, but feel caught by the leader's guide you have to stick to when doing a workshop.

If perhaps your worldview doesn't include freedom in offering with structure and order every so often, how likely have you been to search for solutions to integrate pupil involvement in the current framework?

It is likely to change one's brain design, but if you initially considered what it is. If you are in an atmosphere wherein a focus on student-centered learning makes you feel as if an outside onlooker to the procedure, you may want to think about altering your mental model regarding good learning and the teacher's job.

For one factor, if you believe teachers have to offer order and structure to a learning atmosphere, check out the writings of the father of progressive training, John Dewey, and you will find, and so did he.

Nowadays, how about following a hybrid type - one that includes the best of the demand for order and structure with the best of effective involvement from the learners.

If perhaps your leader's guide has many role-plays and simulations, allow the participants to select the people they think suit them best. If perhaps time permits, break individuals into discussion groups and allow them to build their very simulations and role-plays.

Review whatever lecture notes you have with an eye toward energetic student participation. Time is surely a useful enemy in an innovative classroom but look for chances to pepper your lectures with anecdotes and function examples drawn out of the happenings of the pupils. Search for the right opportunities to disrupt the lecture with open-ended, thought-provoking questions.

To sum up, before rejecting or accepting an instructional technique, examine your beliefs about the correct job of both the teacher and the student in learning.

Made in the USA
Coppell, TX
07 December 2019

12564731R00108